The Future of the Economy

As the pace of economic change seems only to quicken, including rapid technological advance, today's advanced economies face uncertainty from a number of directions, most of which have the potential to change established modes of thinking and the institutional arrangements that underpin basic economic organization. Labor-saving technological advances are accompanied by risks to jobs due to automation. Work is being made more insecure for a wide variety of workers and skill levels because of shifting capital–labor relationships. Regulatory systems are scrambling to adapt to new technologies in infrastructure planning or to the classification of workers under rapidly proliferating "alternative work arrangements." Even the ties that bind groups of countries together in often long-standing bilateral and multilateral trade relationships are increasingly under strain with the rise of populist economic nationalism in some of the world's largest economies. Crucial changes are taking place that risk eroding structures of opportunity, as well as public confidence in the institutions charged with economic policy making in many countries. The expert views contained in this book will be valuable to the reader studying or working on the many overlapping issues of economy, technology, and society and thus looking for insights into some of the most pertinent topics in today's advanced economies.

Taking a multidimensional view, this book synthesizes the main issues and dilemmas facing the economy of the future, seeks to frame the trade-offs in policy terms, while also advancing the discussion toward recommendations and solutions. It focuses on the intersection of work, technology, society, infrastructure, and the economic role of government. In this way, the book is centered on some of the most tangible areas of economic structure that reproduce the gains of growth, but it also addresses matters related to the distribution effects and measures that can produce more inclusive and productive outcomes, including the fundamental role of policy and regulation.

John Powers is Research Fellow at the Lee Kuan Yew Centre for Innovative Cities, Singapore University of Design and Technology, Singapore.

Vikram Khanna is Associate Editor at the *Business Times*, Singapore.

Routledge Studies in the Modern World Economy

Human Services and Long-term Care
A Market Model
Yoshihiko Kadoya

China and Japan in the Global Economy
Edited by Tomoo Kikuchi and Masaya Sakuragawa

Exports, Trade Policy and Economic Growth in Eras of Globalization
Edward M. Feasel

Chinese Trade
Trade Deficits, State Subsidies and the Rise of China
Rich Marino

The Evolution of Economic Wellbeing
Progress-Driven Economic Policies in the Era of Globalization
Zuhayr Mikdashi

Entrepreneurship and Local Economic Development
A Comparative Perspective on Entrepreneurs, Universities and Governments
Edited by Bruno Dallago and Ermanno Tortia

The Future of the Economy
East–West Perspectives on Pathways Through Disruption
John Powers and Vikram Khanna

For more information about this series, please visit: www.routledge.com/Routledge-Studies-in-the-Modern-World-Economy/book-series/SE0432

The Future of the Economy

East–West Perspectives on Pathways
Through Disruption

John Powers and Vikram Khanna

Routledge
Taylor & Francis Group

LONDON AND NEW YORK

First published 2019 by Routledge

2 Park Square, Milton Park, Abingdon, Oxfordshire OX14 4RN

52 Vanderbilt Avenue, New York, NY 10017

Routledge is an imprint of the Taylor & Francis Group, an informa business

First issued in paperback 2020

British Library Cataloguing-in-Publication Data
A catalogue record for this book is available from the British Library

Library of Congress Cataloging-in-Publication Data
Names: Powers, John (John Clancy), author. | Khanna, Vikram, 1956- author.
Title: The future of the economy : east-west perspectives on pathways
    through disruption / John Powers and Vikram Khanna.
Description: New York : Routledge, 2019. | Series: Routledge studies
    in the modern world economy ; 181 | Includes bibliographical
    references and index.
Identifiers: LCCN 2018031349 | ISBN 9781138495753 (hardback) |
    ISBN 9781351023580 (e-book)
Subjects: LCSH: Economic forecasting. | Business forecasting. |
    Economic forecasting—Asia. | Business forecasting—Asia. |
    Asia—Economic conditions—21st century.
Classification: LCC HB3730 .P643 2019 | DDC 330.01/12—dc23
LC record available at https://lccn.loc.gov/2

ISBN: 978-1-138-49575-3 (hbk)
ISBN: 978-0-367-48450-7 (pbk)

Typeset in Times New Roman
by Apex CoVantage, LLC

Contents

Foreword

In 2014, the Lee Kuan Yew Centre for Innovative Cities, a center of excellence in the Singapore University of Technology and Design, launched a research project on The Future of Cities. This forward-looking project focused on Singapore's challenges and future readiness using a rough 25-year time horizon. Singapore is both a city and city-state. The conclusions illustrate some city issues and country issues and would be of interest globally.

The studies were evidence-based and sought to examine the policies implemented, drivers of change, and trends on the horizon and impact. Seven studies were designated to examine "The Future of the Economy," "Future Society," "Data Economy," "Future Transport Policy," "Future Urban Typologies," "Living with Technology," and "Sustainable Futures."

"The Future of the Economy" was the first study to be completed. An international roundtable was organized in January 2017, bringing international experts, high-level Singapore government officials, leading Singapore companies, academics, and the World Bank to focus on the topic of the future of work and the future of the economy facing technology disruption. The Roundtable considered wider issues such as challenges of productivity, infrastructure for the future, inclusive growth, and the role of the state.

It is the objective of the Lee Kuan Yew Centre for Innovative Cities to regularly hold roundtables, workshops, and colloquiums to discuss critical issues of the times that cities and societies are grappling with. We held the first international roundtable on "Data. Social Behaviour. Policy." in 2015. "The Future of the Economy" was our second Roundtable. An international colloquium on "Ageing, Spatial Planning and Social Change" was also held in 2017. We are proud to present the report coming out from the International Roundtable on "The Future of the Economy." It is more than a summary of the workshop. New ideas have been worked on that broadened and enriched the original discussions. We believe this is a useful contribution to understanding this topic.

Chan Heng Chee
Ambassador-at-Large and Chairman
Lee Kuan Yew Centre for Innovative Cities
Singapore University of Technology and Design

Preface

What are some of the major trends and drivers of change in today's advanced economies? Even as the term "disruption," simply ubiquitous these days, appears to announce new challenges for established modes of production, for labor markets, and even for governments seeking to provide better services and opportunities for citizens, more conventional issues and problems such as inequality, how to deliver growth through higher productivity, and responding to infrastructure needs are being reshaped and posed as new challenges. These are some of the areas that were the subject of an international roundtable on the Future of the Economy held in Singapore (at the Regent Hotel) on 24–25 January 2017, organized by the Lee Kuan Yew Centre for Innovative Cities (LKY-CIC) at the Singapore University of Technology and Design. This event stemmed from a 22-month research study pertaining to the Future of the Economy in Singapore, managed by John Powers (Research Fellow at the LKY-CIC), that is part of the Centre's broader Future of Cities Project, which has been funded by Singapore's National Research Foundation and the Ministry of National Development. With so much change occurring in advanced economies that has great potential to alter long-standing economic and social arrangements, not the least of which is a move in some of the world's largest economies toward more professed economic nationalism, we felt an international roundtable would be an opportune setting in which to reflect on these issues globally.

The roundtable was organized around five sessions that were conceived to be broad enough to allow a wide range of perspectives but that were also centered on some key subject areas in order to advance focused discussion in specific areas. The sessions were (1) future of work: reexamining employment and skills, (2) new growth industries and the challenge of productivity, (3) inclusive growth and managing trade-offs, (4) infrastructure for the future, and (5) the role of government in the future of the economy. The event was opened by Minister for Higher Education Ong Ye Kung, who delivered an address that touched on many of the challenges Singapore and other advanced economies are facing. The minister emphasized how the pursuit of new sources of growth must draw upon existing assets as well as forging stronger linkages across the economy in order to do more with less, especially labor, as well as making every effort to promote broadly shared growth and opportunity. The roundtable brought together academics from within Singapore as well as from Canada, the United Kingdom, and the United States; senior government officials from Singapore; and several important industry representatives, in addition to representatives from international agencies like the World Bank.

This publication represents an outcome of all the sessions, presentations, and discussions that took place over the two days. However, it also advances and further develops many of the issues raised through our own additional reading and thinking. As such, this work should be seen as a blended narrative of the various sessions of the roundtable and the themes discussed under each, along with additional inputs to push some of these ideas further and link them to broader academic or policy debates. It is not a verbatim account of the presentations of the different speakers or of interventions made during subsequent discussions. Care has been taken not to attribute our own thinking to those of the speakers at the roundtable but rather to expand upon some of the ideas, themes, and critical issues raised during the two-day event for which limited time may have precluded more substantive reflection on the issues at hand.

Notwithstanding the diversity of the speakers and topics addressed during the roundtable and in these subsequent chapters, many of the issues we raise come back to some similarly grouped themes. These include how to make sense of the impact of technological change on social and economic structure; the connection between innovative activity and productivity for economic growth; the main factors that seem to be driving increases in the socioeconomic disparity in many economies; institutional approaches that can support enhanced social inclusion; evolving labor market structure and the changing nature of skills and employment; design and governance challenges surrounding better infrastructure systems (new and existing), including processes of citizen engagement linked to infrastructure planning; and key policy changes for government to promote more broad-based growth and economic robustness. In addition to the chapters on these topics, there is a final chapter that discusses many of the issues raised during the roundtable, which are covered more from a Western perspective, and that addresses their implications for some of Asia's advanced economies and what it may mean for the Asian developmental state.

1 Future of work

Reexamining employment and skills

OBJECTIVE

What are the main drivers of change in today's workplace? Even as much of the attention is centered on the wide-ranging impacts of labor-saving technological advance and the prospects for automation, other important changes are reshaping the demand and supply of workers and changing the nature of work itself. These include changing capital–labor relationships and the rise of "alternative" work arrangements, as well as emerging labor market mismatches in many economies that reflect new perceptions about how to get ahead in today's economy. How are these challenges to be confronted, and what changes to our institutions and policies may be necessary to meet the challenge?

In their seminal study on the future of work, economics professors Lawrence Katz of Harvard University and Alan Krueger of Princeton University released the startling finding that 94% of the approximately 10 million net new jobs created in the United States from 2005 to 2015 came from what they called "alternative work arrangements," or "non-standard work," with a particularly sharp increase in the share of workers being hired through contract firms or staffing agencies (Katz and Krueger, 2016). They found from their survey of contingent workers (the RAND–Princeton Contingent Worker Survey) that the percentage of workers engaged in such arrangements – variously defined as temporary help agency workers, on-call workers, contract company workers, and independent contractors or freelancers – rose from 10.7% of total national employment at the beginning of 2005 to 15.8% by the end of 2015. The change is all the more significant because there had been almost no such increase in the previous decade between 1995 and 2005.

There are two broad categories of nonstandard work: online gig work (as exemplified by the taxi company Uber), which is conducted through third-party online platforms, and offline alternative work, driven by companies hiring workers through staffing agencies. While both categories grew, offline contract work accelerated faster, having jumped by about 50% from 2005 to 2015. The overall size of the workforce engaged in alternative work is disputed, mainly due to differences in definition; however, Katz and Krueger again estimate that this workforce, both online and offline, accounts for roughly 16% of total U.S. employment.[1]

Why "alternative work" is growing

The growth of alternative work arrangements is driven by forces on both the demand and supply sides. On the demand side, companies find that relying on temporary workers helps cut costs in terms of pay and benefits. Competitive contracting typically leads to lower wage costs than traditional wage setting. Contract workers also enable companies to easily downsize or increase their head count in response to changes in market demand for their products or services and thus to cushion a company's full-time employees from demand shocks. Some analysts also point out that changes in the use of contractors appear to be less costly to a firm's reputation as an employer than layoffs of full-time employees (Halonen-Akatwijuka and Hart, 2016). On the supply side, Katz and Krueger suggest that shifts in the composition of the workforce might explain some of the rise in alternative work. Such arrangements are more common among older and more educated workers, while minorities, another group among which alternative work arrangements are common, have grown as a proportion of the workforce. Rising demand for flexible work hours and concerns about work–life balance are other reasons suggested by researchers, although as Katz and Krueger point out that these are unlikely to be the main causes as staffing firms and temp agencies account for about half the growth in alternative work arrangements over the period covering 2005–2015.

Technology has also helped facilitate the rise of the alternative work-force. The proliferation of social professional networks and online job portals (including for professionals, such as LinkedIn) has eased the task of connecting gig workers with employers. Staffing firms also maintain large databases of workers who may be available for contract assignments. Finally, researchers suggest that the Great Recession of 2008–2009, which led to double-digit unemployment in the United States, might have pushed many workers to seek part-time jobs. However, Katz and Krueger point out that "to the extent this is the case, then one might expect a return to a lower percentage of workers employed in alternative work arrangements over time, as the effects of the recession continue to fade." This does not appear to have happened, suggesting this not a temporary phenomenon.

David Weil, who is professor of management at Boston University's Questrom School of Business, studied these same labor market developments extensively and also has practical policy experience dealing with these issues, having served as the administrator of the Wage and Hour Division (WHD) of the U.S. Department of Labor under the Barack Obama administration from 2014 to January 2017. The WHD's mandate is to promote and enforce compliance with U.S. labor law and standards.

Professor Weil provided some key illustrations of areas where alternative work arrangements, primarily third-party contracting, are not only commonplace in today's economy but are also leading to some unstable and sometimes harmful labor market outcomes. He cited the hotel industry and pointed out that barely 5% of hotels are managed by the owners of the brand, such as Hyatt, Marriott, or the Four Seasons. The rest are run by management companies. They in turn rely on staffing agencies to provide workers for a whole range of services including cleaning, food and beverage, landscaping, housekeeping, security, and more. Typically, the employees performing these functions come not from a single employer but from as many as 12–15 different contractors and subcontractors. The glue binding these employees together is an often highly specific set of standards set by the brand owner. The logistics industry is another case in point. Large distribution centers owned by companies like Amazon and Walmart typically consist of an "incoming dock" that receives goods delivered by suppliers. The goods are then sorted, in sorting areas, into different categories and in turn conveyed to an "outgoing dock" before they are delivered to individual stores and homes. The various parts of this supply chain are run by different companies relying on staffing agencies for their workers. Similar arrangements are increasingly prevalent in a wide array of activities and professions, including agriculture, shipbuilding, assembly line manufacturing, the food and beverage industry, IT services, retail, law, journalism, and medicine. Although the focus on third-party contracting and alternative work has often been on low-skilled, low-wage work, this is also beginning to change to include more high-skilled white-collar work.

Stressing how such work practices have some serious consequences, such as weaker health and safety conditions for the workers involved, the risks are often minimized or ignored as the web of contracting grows larger and the burden of responsibility becomes less clear as it is shifted from contractor to contractor. Workers are often denied the benefits, such as health care, vacation pay, overtime pay, and pensions, provided to full-time employees, and they often do not even get proper safety training.

Describing this process by which more and more employment has become subject to this increasing precariousness, Weil speaks of the modern workplace as becoming "fissured," which stems from how large "lead" firms are increasingly shedding employment to increasingly smaller and less stable contractors, subcontractors, and a host of third-party managers. This phenomenon is in several important ways driven by the capital markets, which are exerting pressure on these lead firms, which have global brand name recognition in the marketplace, to focus on their "core competencies." It is this double-edged process – by which large firms contract out more and more functions that used to be carried out within the firm to outside parties, which often in turn subcontract that work to still others with an accompanying deterioration in the wage and benefit structure for the workers involved – that Weil describes as the "fissured workplace," as outlined in his 2014 book by the same name. On a macro level, fissuring leads to rising inequalities, driven by differences in wages between full-time staff and contract workers, and this is further exacerbated by the absence of unionization among the latter group.

Addressing the historical context is important here because the accuracy of a juxtaposition of an unstable fissured workplace in the contemporary context against a relatively secure employment relationship in large vertically integrated firms preceding it may be out of line with some of the historical evolution of large corporate structures, particularly in Western advanced economies. Professor Susan Fainstein reacts to the characterization that what preceded the rise of workplace fissuring, namely the idea that large firms with their large internal labor markets employing everyone from senior management to the rank-and-file workers, down to the janitor and the cafeteria worker, was in fact a relatively brief period in industrial history, particularly in the United States. Thus, the idea that the rise of alternative workplace arrangements is a move away from a stable and long-standing past might be a bit of a mischaracterization of these economic transformations.

As to the measures needed to deal with the problem of fissuring, Weil suggested that employer education is an important first step. In an interview with *The Washington Post*, he said, "I think the majority of noncompliance that we see is people just not getting what the law is, and what their responsibilities are under it" (DePillis, 2016). While he stressed the need for enforcement and proposing that companies take more responsibility for their contract workers, which is seldom the case today, client companies and the staffing agencies that supply them should be considered "joint employers" and thus be mutually liable for violations of workers' rights. Among the most egregious of violations, according to Weil, is the misclassification of workers (*Wall Street Journal*, 2015). By misclassifying workers as "independent contractors," even when they are employed for long periods, companies can avoid paying benefits such as Social Security, Medicare, and overtime, in addition to paying lower wages.[2]

However, Dave DeSario, who runs a group called the Alliance for the American Temporary Workforce, argues that the "joint employer" solution is unlikely to work because staffing agencies and clients end up blaming each other when something goes wrong. Without a union, temporary workers are not likely to get the representation that would enable them to pursue legitimate claims of labor or workplace violations. He calls for more transparency in the safety records of staffing agencies and for more information on how many of those temporary workers go on to find permanent jobs. Lawrence Katz suggests more fundamental reforms are necessary, saying, "We need to re-think labor laws." He argues there should be more consideration to whether independent contractors should have the right to organize and to how benefits can be extended to workers who do not have a single stable source of employment. Katz also calls for a safety net and employer policies and regulations that allow workers to have security while at the same time being able to operate in a labor market where they may do many jobs at the same time or across the span of their careers (Gardner, 2016).

A key challenge for policy makers, then, is to craft laws and regulations which, on the one hand, enable companies to outsource some of their job functions in order to remain competitive, while ensuring that part-time and gig workers enjoy adequate protection, security, and at least some benefits throughout their careers, on the other.

Technology and the future of work

Technology has always had a profound impact on the nature of work across industries and occupations, and the impact of technological change on the labor market has long fascinated social scientists. In the 20th century, there have been evaluations of the job impact of countless innovations ranging from assembly line manufacturing and agricultural mechanization to container shipping, computers, the Internet, among many others. Today, increasing attention has been on technologies that intuitively seem directly connected to the future of work, such as robotics, 3D printing, artificial intelligence (AI), and digitization, all of which can be said to fall under the broad category of workforce automation.

These technologies are already up and running and in many areas surpass human capabilities. Computers already outperform humans in some of the most intellectually challenging games such as chess, Go, Jeopardy, backgammon, and poker. Some might say driverless cars are already better drivers than the average human. Surgical robots, operated via remote control, can already perform low-risk operations. AI-enhanced computer systems are beginning to interpret results of X-rays much faster than radiologists, pick stocks better than stock analysts, and do legal due diligence faster than teams of paralegals. These examples can be multiplied. The ability of these new technological advances to penetrate into the domain of "non-routine" forms of labor is clearly going to increase the scope for disruptions in the labor market in the years ahead.

One of the more comprehensive studies of the implications of workplace automation was carried out by the McKinsey Global Institute (MGI) covering 46 countries representing about 80% of the global workforce. The study examined more than 2,000 work activities and attempted to measure the technical feasibility of automating each of them ("Technology, Jobs and the Future of Work," 2017). Emphasizing current technologies, the study stressed that fewer than 5% of today's jobs can be fully automated, although this figure could be more on the order of 15–20% for work in "medium-skilled categories." However, the concept of partial automation is where we can see a far greater scope in the range of functions that can be disrupted by new technologies. The study finds that approximately 60% of all jobs have at least 30% of activities within them that are technically automatable. A skills bias in terms of how workers may be impacted from the advance of automation is likely. Less-skilled workers working with technology may be able to achieve higher output and register greater productivity gains but are also susceptible to experiencing wage pressure given their larger representation in the workforce in most advanced economies.

Although there are big differences in automation potential across countries depending on the structure of economies, wage levels, and the size and dynamics of the workforce, the adaptation of current technologies to whole or partial automation could affect about half of the world economy, according to the MGI study. This would entail roughly 1.2 billion employees and approximately $14.6 trillion in wages. Even with the technical feasibility to automate jobs increasing all the time, this does not necessarily mean that such widespread impacts will actually occur. Other important factors can moderate the pace and extent of automation in the workplace. These include the cost of deploying automatable technologies, existing labor costs, regulatory frameworks surrounding work and the workplace, and social pressures pertaining to the acceptability of automation in the workplace. Even while technologies might replace some jobs, they also create new jobs and income possibilities in old and new industries.

Jobs versus tasks

In any discussion of automation and jobs, an important insight often overlooked is the importance of distinguishing between "jobs" and "tasks." The view that jobs will be either automated away or not is rather simplistic. As consultants Malcom Frank, Paul Roehrig, and Ben Pring of the global technology consultancy Cognizant put it, "Any knowledge job is a collection of tasks. Some of these tasks are ripe for automation, while others never will be" (Frank et al., 2017). Forrester Research, which has undertaken extensive studies of the automation of jobs, points out that "the greatest change to the workforce will be in job transformation, leading to redeployment and responsibility-shifting impacting the part of the worker." Consider the example of cable television technicians whose work has expanded considerably beyond simply connecting coaxial cables to poles and into households, as it used to be several decades ago, and now involves setting up Internet services, wireless routers, and home security equipment.

The transformation of jobs as a result of automation is, of course, nothing new. For example, the introduction of tractors early in the last century first in the developed world and later in the developing world dramatically reduced the need for labor in plowing land but vastly increased the number of jobs needed for threshing and harvesting. How innovation creates as well as destroys jobs is difficult to predict given that the rate and direction of technical advance is far from being a linear progression. For example, the introduction of automated teller machines (ATMs) in the 1970s initially displaced some bank tellers but significantly reduced the cost of running bank branches, enabling banks to open more branches, thus creating more employment. While the negative impact of automation on jobs is relatively immediate and obvious, its positive impact is often less clear and can occur in other areas. As Joel Mokyr, an economic historian at Northwestern University, put it: "Imagine trying to tell someone a century ago that her great-grandchildren would be video-game designers or cybersecurity specialists. These are jobs that nobody in the past would have predicted" (*Economist*, 2016). But the net effect of automation on jobs is difficult to estimate. While on the one hand, jobs might be created in the future that cannot today be predicted, there is also the question of whether these jobs-to-be-created would exceed those lost to automation and over what time period. How rapidly organizations adopt, deploy, and customize new technologies and what regulatory issues they will face are also difficult to foresee.

In recent years, some of the most dramatic technological advances have come from the field of artificial intelligence (AI). As presented by Jonathan Woetzel, senior partner and director at the McKinsey Global Institute (MGI), AI has been through ups and downs, often promising more than it delivered. However, over the last decade it has witnessed a revival, driven partly by exponential increases in computing power. This has enabled vast amounts of digital data to be both collected and analyzed, enabling innovations in other areas such as autonomous vehicles, the Internet of Things, and personalized medicine, among many others.

Relying on an approach that aims to provide a more fine-grained analysis of where AI can likely impact the workplace, emphasis is placed on where demonstrated technologies powered by AI affect various occupations. Occupations are disaggregated into sets of activities and then further into human capabilities. As to AI's impact on jobs, the MGI research pointed to some 800 occupations, 2,000 activities, and 18 core human capabilities that could potentially be affected. Regarding capabilities, these include sensory perception, cognition, physical and motor skills, and social and emotional sensing. The impact of automation on jobs needs to be considered precisely in terms of such capabilities, and from this perspective, it is evident that while AI-driven automation will affect all occupations to a degree, it will surely impact some more than others. The work of psychiatrists, legislators, and artists, for example, are less amenable to automation, but so are some lower-wage jobs such as landscaping, cooking, and forms of craftsmanship. On the professional side, some work such as radiology, investment analysis, and certain forms of journalism are already being automated, and surely more will come. Overall, the McKinsey Global Institute estimates that just over half of the U.S. economy is driven by activities that could be potentially automated. Similar effects will be felt globally, particularly in the United States, China, Japan (all early adopters), and India, which between them have more than a billion workers.

Echoing the MGI research, a detailed report by the National Academies of Science, Engineering and Medicine, released in April 2017, asserts that opportunities for digitizing and automating tasks "are far from exhausted" (*Information Technology and the US Workforce*, 2017). It focuses on how more cognitive tasks, from language processing to advanced forms of pattern recognition, will allow AI advances to make their way into high-skilled occupations, undoubtedly changing the nature of work and perhaps also significantly altering the skills bias alluded to earlier. Robotic automation will also surely advance, according to the report, including in areas that have not thus far felt the impact of such technologies. Over the next decade, self-driving cars, already being deployed in various prototype stages in numerous country contexts, will likely become more widespread, bringing major impacts on jobs in the transportation industry.

Despite the nature and extent of these advancements in AI and in related areas of robotics and machine learning, automation has proceeded far more slowly than it could. Even in an advanced postindustrial economy like the United States, only about 18% of the current digitization potential has been reached. According to Mr. Woetzel, "There is a huge long tail of industry that has not been digitized," including large parts of major industries such as retail, health care, and construction. Job automation on a scale commensurate with what is technologically feasible is thus likely to take decades, although policy makers can certainly hasten the process by supporting the development of automation technologies and encouraging meaningful life-long learning initiatives that will allow for smoother labor substitution and transitions. However, the potential of AI-driven automation is subject to some interesting caveats.

Automation, past, and future

Highlighting what is called the Moravec Paradox (named after Hans Moravec, a robotics scientist and futurist), Ravi Menon, managing director of the Monetary Authority of Singapore, raised an interesting set of points about different sets of skills along a spectrum of complexity and what this may hold for automation and the future of work. Moravec's Paradox pertains to the discovery by artificial intelligence and robotics research-ers that, contrary to traditional assumptions, high-level reasoning requires very little computation but that, conversely, low-level sensorimotor skills – which even children possess – require enormous computational resources. Examples that appear effortless include recognizing a face, catching a ball, judging peoples' motivations, setting a goal, and a variety of visualization, motor, and social skills. These abilities have evolved over many millennia in animals and humans. Moravec's research suggests that the difficulty of reverse-engineering such abilities is roughly proportional to the amount of time taken for them to evolve in humans. By contrast, skills that evolved more recently in historical time, like logic, mathematics, scientific reason-ing, and analytically challenging games, are relatively easier to incorporate into AI systems.

First, Menon pointed out that, while eventually the paradox may be resolved, meaning that the longer evolved skills may also be replicated, the implications suggest that many higher-paid professionals such as stock ana-lysts, engineers, and accountants might be more easily disrupted by AI than some lower-paid professionals such as cooks, gardeners, and social workers, which is consistent with the findings of the MGI research. Second, there is the possibility that recent technological advances, notably digitization, may have a different social and economic impact than past forms of workplace automation. Previous rounds of automation have almost always led to more jobs, higher incomes, and lower inequality, as many technologies in the past tended to substitute for skills, but also creating new demand for skills in other areas has opened up new jobs and applications of human capabilities, even for the less skilled, something historians of technical advance refer to as "technological opportunity" (Rosenberg, 1976; Nelson and Winter, 1982). Citing how Ford's assembly line was basically for unskilled work-ers, Mr. Menon emphasized how the current wave of digitization may be skill-biased, favoring those who can work with new technologies, adding to concerns about job insecurity and inequality. Can education systems keep up, in terms of access and content, with the pace of technology? Whether they can will likely have significant bearing on the evolving structure of inequality and the returns to particular types of work and their underlying skills.

Third, even if as many estimates suggest, roughly 60% of jobs may be automated on the order of about 30%, that still leaves 70% of job content to be performed by humans. The question then becomes how effectively humans can work with machines? How are economies evolving the skills and competencies to work with machines so that human labor inputs and the automated portions can better complement each other to make a job richer and more meaningful?

Lastly, the rise of the service sector is an important phenomenon being experienced in all advanced economies. Major sectoral shifts in employment have happened before. For instance, 150 years ago, more than half of the workforce in many developed economies worked in agriculture, but massive increases in farm productivity led to a shift of millions of workers into the manufacturing sector. Today, agriculture sector employment is a fraction of what it was, and yet the sector produces many more times than what it did in the last century. Is manufacturing the new agriculture? Mr. Menon noted that with automation, manufacturing productivity is rising sharply, requiring fewer workers. However, we all still need to consume. Consumption of a wide range of services will remain a mainstay of our economies; so going forward, domestic tradable and nontradable services will be especially important in a still growing array of sectors.

Skills mismatches and the role of education systems

Given the rapid pace of change, it is not surprising that recent research has found evidence for significant mismatches among skills, jobs, and locations (McKinsey, 2017). Many employers in advanced economies say that they cannot find enough workers with the skills they need. A McKinsey survey of young people and employers in nine countries found that 40% of employers reported a lack of skills the principal reason for unfilled entry-level jobs. The skills gap included not only highly sought-after technical skills relating to STEM (science, technology, engineering, and math) subject knowledge but also interpersonal or basic professional skills such as communication, teamwork, and even punctuality. For their part, 37% of job seekers indicated that their current job does not allow them to fully utilize their skills or provide them with enough of a challenge. McKinsey's report points out that some of these mismatch issues are also substantially locational, with workers unable to be found where they are needed. To some extent, this gap is filled through internal and cross-border migration, but there are obvious limits to this, some of it being the result of tightening government restrictions on migration, even for skilled labor. The political climate across much of Europe to North America has seen immigration become a flash point issue for policy makers and national legislatures and has led to reduced labor market flexibility, and this has had a particularly acute effect on economies confronting aging of the workforce.

Problems of mismatches also raise the issue of the relevance of education systems to changes in labor markets and the needs of employers. This was the focus of Dr. Michael Zibrowius, a labor economist at the Cologne Institute for Economic Research. Addressing the German experience, which is often held up as an interesting international case study with regard to skills acquisition through its long-standing vocational and apprenticeship systems, Zibrowius highlighted three trends. First is a decline in the workforce and a shortage of young people. Youth unemployment in Germany is just 6.7% compared to 10% in the United States and more than 40% in Spain and Greece. Second, mismatches between the educational qualifications of workers and the needs of employers are becoming more significant, similar to McKinsey's findings. Third is the implications of increasing digitization in the workplace. He pointed out that, despite the fact that approximately two-thirds of the German workforce has vocational education, there has been a strong trend toward increasing enrollment in higher education and a consequent decline in apprenticeships over the last 20 years. This gradual decline of demand for vocational education – in a system that is known for a rich set of social institutions and practices that have produced a highly productive layer of the economy in many skilled trades and precision engineering sectors in which lifelong earnings has often exceeded those jobs for which university degrees are more common – is a development that reflects not just mismatches in the German labor market but more fundamental shifts in perfections about work and career aspirations.

In Germany, these developments have led to increasing labor shortages, particularly in vocational areas. For example, companies are finding it hard to recruit refrigeration technicians, operators of agricultural machinery, or geriatric care workers. In the field of mechatronics, only 24 qualified unemployed workers are available for every 100 vacancies. Speaking about labor mismatches, Zibrowius stresses how people are wanting to pursue university degrees even though the labor market is seeking people with vocational expertise. In fact, it is vocationally qualified people with technical skills who tend to be the ones actually driving automation in many industries. Although the unemployment rate for university graduates is low at around 2%, the mismatches raise questions of whether, given the demands of the labor market, it is smarter for people to pursue university degrees. Vocational education provides a good way for a young graduate to start a career, and it need not be regarded as the end of one's education. Dr. Zibrowius suggested that the German experience shows that education systems need to be more permeable so that people can easily shift with less friction from vocational to tertiary education. Students also need better career guidance so they can make choices that correspond to their skills and competencies, as well as the needs of employers. The case of Singapore is also instructive here. In an education (and civil service) system known for its adherence to meritocratic principles, particularly as regards entry into the higher education system, and a consequent rigidity in terms of accessing tertiary education opportunity for those regarded as being on more of a vocational track, the government is increasingly paying much closer attention to creating more avenues of opportunity between different types of institutions of higher learning. This is an important aspect of the government's overall efforts to pursue more inclusive economic growth and social development.

This point about needed shifts in education to support the kinds of skill development to help graduates and workers adapt in the fast-paced labor market of today (and tomorrow) was also advanced by Ravi Menon. There is a need for a shift from content mastery to a capacity to learn and from "learn and earn" to "learn, earn, and learn more." He emphasized how the notion that people should study first and then work for the rest of their working lives is obsolete. Education systems must also consider shifting some of their emphasis away from providing academic qualifications and toward developing and certifying skills, with a particular need for skills that advanced technologies are not able to deliver as yet, such as creativity, complex forms of communication, design-centric thinking, and even empathy. However, employers also need to change, especially in their approaches to hiring, training, and deploying workers. With such new directions, hopefully the enormous technological progress and the transformation of jobs being witnessed today will create the conditions for greater economic abundance, as well as more broadly shared possibilities.

Notes

1 A 2014 study by the Freelancers Union and the online contract work portal Upwork estimated that the freelance workforce (defined as anyone who does contract work, whether or not they have ever filed with the IRS) to be 34% of all workers. In any event, it is a significant part of the workforce. It is also growing in countries other than the United States.
2 Under Weil's direction, the Wage and Hour Division issued detailed guidelines on the legal obligations and responsibilities of employers in this regard. The Division also stepped up its enforcement of laws, including "naming and shaming" egregious violators and ordering the payment of penalties where appropriate.

2 New growth industries and the challenge of productivity

OBJECTIVE

In the oft talked about era of technology disruption, what are the likely sources of productivity-enhancing technological advance, and how will these be reflected in new industries or in transforming existing ones? In what ways might these advances impact output and value creation leading to higher productivity? What might be some of the downsides and trade-offs to consider?

Technology and society: considering the long-run policy implications

The connection between jobs and technical advance seems to be on everyone's mind these days and is the source of much debate, as predicting how far automation, computerization, and advances in artificial intelligence will whittle away at the need for large numbers of workers is something that remains an unanswered question. As Darrel West of the Brookings Institution asserts, autonomous vehicles will someday, perhaps sooner than later, take the jobs of truck and taxi drivers as well as delivery persons, and the issue of how to redeploy displaced workers into new occupational fields remains a central concern for any economy seeking to get more from its workers. Since the end of the recession extending back to 2010, technical advance has contributed strongly to rising output levels in U.S. manufacturing, according to the Bureau of Labor Statistics, but with less input from labor. This certainly constitutes a productivity increase, but it poses a dilemma regarding the pace and the extent of job creation.

Even where there has been substantial job creation in the advanced economies over the last 25 years, a significant share of this increase, as alluded to in the preceding chapter, can be characterized as a relatively new type of employment relationship between large firms and a web of contractors, subcontractors, and third-party managers. Large firms are outsourcing many functions that had formerly been carried out in-house, being "disciplined" in new ways by the pressures of the capital markets to focus on their so-called core business. This has made it continuously easier for capital to shift the responsibilities for delivering work-related social benefits onto smaller and often less stable firms, with the result all too often being a downgrading of the quality and extent of these benefits. Combined with the effects of automation and computerization of workplace tasks and perhaps of whole occupations in the future, the general environment is one of increasing precariousness of work and the overall employment relationship. It is for this reason that West stresses the need for a new social contract surrounding work in an era of rapid technological change.

As demand for STEM-trained workers will surely continue to grow in the years ahead, one of the greatest challenges from a policy standpoint will be to manage the emergence of skills mismatches given not just the rapid pace of technological change but the convergence of new technologies in the workplace that will require fundamentally more multidisciplinary skill sets. This in turn increases the relevance of strong and well-conceived vocational training programs, as well as a rethinking of aspects of the educational system with a stronger emphasis on learning how to learn. Many economies in the years ahead will be reliant on greater proportions of older workers, as is the case in many Asian economies in particular; the ability to upgrade workers' skills with a strong focus on capability development will be an imperative for economies to remain competitive in a global environment characterized by a tightening supply of skilled labor supply. Although there is considerable variation from country to country, there is cause to inquire about the effectiveness of vocational education systems and other programs to retrain for whole new career pathways, as opposed to merely helping retrenched workers access new jobs. The efficacy of these systems is often rooted in the strength of social institutions surrounding the skilled trades and other craft-based industries as in many parts of Europe, but also in Japan, as discussed in the previous chapter.

What is happening to Asia's developmental state in the age of frontier innovation?

The idea of innovation and new growth industries was advanced in the context of late industrialization and especially Asia's developmental state. The region's economic achievements over the last several decades, as is now a well told story, is in large part a story of industrial catchup with the role of the developmental state overcoming many of the coordination problems characteristic of late industrialization. These have been known to include low private savings, dependence on primary products, declining prices for exports with respect to imports (i.e., diminishing terms of trade), small internal markets, high levels of unemployment, limited skills, and few entrepreneurs capable of managing large-scale organizations (Amsden, 1989, 2001). Under such conditions, the debate over the appropriate role for government in the process of economic development has tended to be cast in rather polemic terms, as being a choice between inward versus outward oriented industrialization. Of course, this debate has changed considerably over the intervening decades and has become more centered on government's role in supporting innovation in the context of a more integrated global economy along with the increased segmentation of industrial value chains.

Whereas in earlier stages of industrial development, many of today's now advanced Asian economies were effectively "plugging themselves into" a growing global economy largely on the basis of nonproprietary technology – in other words, on the basis of technologies that had already been substantially commercialized by firms in other regions – the contemporary period is quite different. Operating at or near the world technological frontier, as many of Asia's high-performing economies have been for some years now, a new set of strategic choices confront the developmental state that has been a big part of the growth story. The issue is essentially one of the policies and institutional challenges of promoting sustained innovation and leadership in business firms.

A new strategic choice is argued to be one of allocating resources to spur innovation of a frontier variety in the context of pervasive uncertainty. The economic role of government in promoting advanced industries must therefore contend with managing "primary risk." This refers to the systemic nature of economic uncertainty inherent to new growth industries in which the underlying science and technological base is evolving so rapidly, as well as innovative activity being of such an experimental and complex nature. In relatively smaller economies such as Taiwan, Singapore, and, to a lesser extent, Korea, the challenges of managing this kind of fundamental risk from a public policy standpoint are multifaceted. Even with an oversupply of potential subsidies to allocate toward R&D in any of a number of targeted growth sectors, the dilemma from a policy standpoint is that one is "betting blind," according to Professor Joseph Wong. In other words, the experimental and trial-and-error–ridden nature of many of today's growth industries requires scale on both the input and output sides of innovation, as well as a high tolerance for failure.

This is perhaps nowhere more evident than in one of the 21st century's truly frontier industries, biotechnology and the biomedical sciences. City-regions around the world and indeed national economies are leveraging very substantial assets – financial resources to support research activities, infrastructure development for state-of-the-art facilities, incentives for new business investment, and efforts to expand industry–university collaborations – in order to stake their claim as the next big biotech hub. One of the key issues embedded in this prospect, however, is the need for critical mass in not just research activity but also in terms of clinicians, medical schools, firms, investors, and other complementary actors in order to create crucial feedback effects between suppliers of upstream research and other intermediate and downstream users who also input important information into the process of innovation that may lead to new commercialization opportunities. Building critical mass is all the more significant given the high failure rates inherent to such science-driven experimental activities aimed essentially at discovery. The successful pursuit of these outcomes is not a clear function of the amount of financial resources invested and other factors on the input side, although it is unlikely the growth of the industry would flourish without substantial and sustained resource commitments. In smaller open economies like some of those in East and Southeast Asia, this can be a high-risk endeavor.

A new role for the developmental state, therefore, can be cast as a change from being less of a resource distributor and decision maker to that of risk manager. It must take on the fundamental uncertainty of placing bets on innovating at the world technological frontier in industries that have extraordinary growth potential but highly variable rates at which innovative effort yields the successful commercialization of scientific research. The dilemma is perhaps best understood as a problem about screening methodologies as it regards weighing the possible payoff functions among different R&D projects by a firm. This is characterized in terms of the direction of innovative activity and the level of effort to allocate to it. Screening will typically take place on a spectrum between projects that present the greatest commercial viability on one hand and those projects that contain the most interesting scientific or technological possibilities on the other. Although the former is generally a safer approach, the latter can produce very sizable payoffs, if it pays off at all.[1] Growing successful, innovation-leading companies that can contribute significantly to new high-value employment creation and thus broader economic growth is, to a significant degree, a numbers game about maximizing economic and technological opportunity across an array of innovative activities and actors in a given industry. This is particularly the case in sectors that are fraught with uncertain market outcomes (Rosenberg, 1996). From a public policy standpoint, the parallels to placing bets is quite germane, and the long-term view required and uncertain payoffs on the output side, at least in the short and medium terms, require significant patience on the part of government planners and the management of almost certain policy tensions about the effectiveness of public support to science-driven industries.

Arguments about the relative autonomy of economic planners and their being insulated from political pressures to deliver outcomes, given sustained high levels of public funds committed to research activity and industrial development efforts, have perhaps never been more pertinent for pursuing the long-term view that is surely needed to help build critical mass in innovation-driven growth industries. This has been a hallmark of the developmental state in previous decades and will likely be an important feature in the years ahead as well albeit in different institutional configurations. However, relative autonomy is no guarantee that bets made will pay off in this context, where experimental processes of R&D in which the underlying science base is evolving so rapidly, can produce such variability in commercializable output. This is likely to be the case despite the scale of investments often required on the input side. Making this risk management role for the developmental state more effective in its support for frontier innovation would be an institutional mechanism that can help socialize losses without reducing incentives for experimental activities oriented to discovery as well as commercialization. Examples might include funding support for industry–university research collaborations, grant support for firms that have passed Phase I clinical trials or have reached some other advanced prototype stage of development, or tax concessions for firms that have proven robust R&D platforms.[2]

New possibilities for productivity from mobile Internet technology

When one considers all the ways the Internet and mobile communications technologies have changed the way we live, work, play, and learn, one must ask how will this continue to evolve? Will the next wave of innovations in the Internet-of-Things, e-commerce, and a variety of web-based applications be as impactful as what we have seen in the last 20 years? One need not look very far to see people living and working on their smart phones and various mobile devices like never before. The computing power that is now available at one's fingertips has created dramatic new opportunities for transmitting ideas, making critical communications and more informed decisions, concluding transactions, querying data, and just generally enhancing human connectivity. It becomes increasingly more difficult to imagine how we managed to make our way to new places or buy movie tickets before this explosion of web-based commerce and the IT revolution of the last couple of decades.

Considering that approximately 3 billion people today have Internet access, according to Google's Caesar Sengupta, at the rate at which global Internet penetration is occurring, it is likely that another billion users will be added in the next few years alone. The potential this holds for a further expansion of not just the user base but also the innovation and development of new applications and services to cater to that user base is of great significance in the way the Internet and the ease of communication will continue to transform human social and economic interaction. Speaking of an epochal shift in the way that information is stored, accessed, and transmitted, Mr. Sengupta asserts that today's smart phones are as powerful as some of the most advanced personal computers of a decade or more ago, with similarly powerful accessories such as cameras and internal processing power to download and store data at ever more rapid speeds.

Users themselves in many of the world's fast growing markets, such as in East and Southeast Asia but in many other areas of the world as well, are part of a younger generation whose first experience with information technology is through a mobile device or smart phone as opposed to a personal computer. Living in rapidly urbanizing environments, many of them have low incomes at present, but the disposable portion of their income is projected to grow in the years ahead, likely making them a sophisticated and valuable group of users in the near future. Their active inclusion in the mobile Internet space is surely likely to influence the rate and direction of further technical advance, particularly as this era of development of new applications is far more diffuse and democratized than in previous stages of development in information technology. This has created considerable scope for active feedback processes among users, developers, and service providers and is enabling firms and public sector institutions to manage assets, optimize performance, and create new business models. The way that technological domains and their industrial applications, in this case the Internet of Things, cloud computing, and mobile Internet in particular, are converging is continuously expanding new technological as well as market opportunities. The degree of digitization across a country's economic and social sectors, including the public sector, is an important factor in setting the stage for productivity growth in subsequent periods of technology deployment and adoption.

To what extent may market size effect influence an economy's ability to be a leader in producing high-value products and services for this rapidly expanding and converging mobile Internet, computing, and information technology industry? The case of Southeast Asia is noteworthy in that, if one were to draw a concentric circle radiating outward at a distance roughly equivalent to six hours' flying time with Singapore at its center, this would capture approximately a full one-half of the world's population, according to Mr. Sengupta. It would also contain some of the world's fastest growing economies and a significant portion of the young demographic previously mentioned. In developing products and leading firms for this Southeast

Asian market and the broader Asia Pacific region, an economy like Singapore's must leverage and continue to develop its assets. These include but are certainly not limited to the following: being the regional headquarters for numerous technology multinationals; having a world-class education system; being a robust national platform for R&D, including a focus on developing capabilities in deep data analysis and machine learning; as well as a probusiness and English-speaking legal and regulatory environment backed up by a government with a long-standing commitment to the rule of law.

In the commercial and legal environment, given the pace of technological change in these information technology industries, modernizing the regulatory framework requires a recognition that countries are also competing in the regulatory sphere. This requires a continuous effort at innovation across the public sector and ensuring that regulatory frameworks are supportive of technological change, including being as adaptive as possible to market disruption. Consequently, leading an effort aimed at creating a common digital market in one of the most dynamic regions of the world, regardless of what slowdown may be occurring at present, would be a key policy step geared to overcoming the limitations of a small domestic market, facilitating broader market access, and thereby helping to grow e-commerce companies with significant scale and market reach.

Technical advance, work, and productivity growth

The previous chapter explored issues in workplace automation and the importance of relating currently available technologies to the specific activities, tasks, and human capabilities involved in contemporary work in order to meaningfully tackle the question of job disruption brought on by technological advance. Another important facet of this question involves the same need to disaggregate work into its various elements for the purpose of studying not just labor displacement but also whether productivity is increasing as a result, as is often expected. Exploring this intersection running between human capabilities, work activities, and occupations is very much at the heart of the matter when it comes to technological change and its impact on the labor force and the changing nature of work itself. The introduction of new technologies to the workplace and to existing work practices is continually changing the functional and the substantive aspects of tasks and activities that comprise work in the contemporary capitalist system. Much of this is not the wholesale destruction of jobs per se but rather the partial automation of work and the consequent reshaping of the often routine aspects of work but of increasingly the less-routine as well. Where these impacts play out in the workforce will have a lot to say not just about labor disruption but also where jobs and occupations are enhanced through the combination of human labor and technology leading to productivity increases. The challenge of being able to make assessments and even projections about the ways currently available technologies, much less ones on the near horizon, can disrupt work tasks and activities across an array of occupations and sectors requires access to highly detailed and up-to-date information. This must be of the sort that brings together job and activity requirements, on the one hand, with the cognitive, skill, behavioral, social, and experience-based context in which those activities and jobs take place, on the other.

Even though such a set of rich occupational data does in fact exist – at least in the United States in the form of the Occupation Information Network (O*NET), which is the online successor to the long-standing Dictionary of Occupational Titles (DOT) developed under sponsorship of the U.S. Department of Labor and its Employment and Training Administration – the work of relating this fine-grained occupation data to questions of automation and the advance of artificial intelligence in the workplace remains a significant challenge. The work of MIT economist David Autor and his colleagues has sought to empirically examine the direction of technical advance from a skills perspective (Autor et al., 2003), specifically how the decline of computer capital – the relative price of introducing computerized technology, or, in a word, automation – has affected the nature and extent of task input for routine and nonroutine forms of labor over a period of almost four decades (1960–1998). Employing data from the DOT and survey data from the Census and the Current Population Survey, their central conclusions point to substitution effects away from routine labor in industries undergoing rapid computerization, as well as a generalized shifting of work-related tasks toward nonroutine forms of labor across all education levels. In other words, jobs and occupations that are less prone to being codified as a discrete set of rule-based activities, irrespective of education level, were less susceptible to automation. This conclusion is also reached by economists Frank Levy and Richard Murnane in their book *The New Division of Labor*.

More recently, some of this work has been expanded upon in new but related directions, often using data from the Annual Survey of Manufacturers in the United States, to empirically investigate claims about whether IT-intensive industries (e.g., following a measure of IT-intensity, those that have been relatively aggressive in adopting IT technology in manufacturing activity) are in fact achieving higher than normal productivity gains (Acemoglu et al., 2014). The authors are in many ways responding to others[3] who assert technological advance and digital automation to be leading transformations that will lead to a substantially and presumably permanent smaller role in the economy for labor, as well as to the suggestion that this latter constitutes evidence for the resolution of the Solow Paradox – the famous statement by Robert Solow that "computers are found everywhere except in the productivity statistics" made in the late 1980s. The authors (Acemoglu et al., 2014) find that the evidence for a pervasive IT-driven revolution in the economy producing outsized productivity gains and thus driving the declining labor share in manufacturing, especially in IT-intensive manufacturing, is not all that strong. Where they do find stronger than normal productivity increases, it is more common for them to be driven by declining relative output and even steeper declines in manufacturing employment (which can register in the data as a productivity increase). This is not the kind of evidence to definitively say that computerization, the introduction of AI, and the automation of work have resolved once and for all the Solow Paradox. Surely, technological change will continue to influence relative prices of automation that will in turn lead to more deployment of new advances within the workplace, altering the nature of routine and nonroutine forms of labor. Further studies will be needed using the kind of fine-grained occupational and skill-related data contained in sources like O*NET but also with an explicit effort to more rigorously equate existing technological domains to specific occupations, activities, and tasks within those occupations and further still to different categories of human work-related capabilities, as in the MGI research alluded to in the previous chapter.

Notes

1 For a more thorough discussion of these issues, please see Nelson and Winter (1982) and, more recently, Powers (2013).
2 For a more thorough discussion of policy-based approaches to support the goals of broad-based innovative activity, see OECD (2010).
3 In particular, the work of Brynjolfsson and McAfee (2011) and their widely read short book, *Race Against the Machine: How the Digital Revolution Is Accelerating Innovation, Driving Productivity, and Irreversibly Transforming Employment and the Economy*, which is a provocative statement about what they see as an inexorable trend of digital automation across many sectors of the economy and aspects of the workplace that is responsible for productivity gains that exceed more aggregate measures.

3 Inclusive growth and managing trade-offs

OBJECTIVE

The long-standing reciprocal tension between growth and equity is a debate that has had many incarnations over succeeding generations, but it is one that has taken on renewed significance in an international context of dramatic increases in income inequality in recent decades. Where are the current lines of the debate being drawn, and what are some of the causal factors? Where it has been less severe, what have been some of the policy factors that have been instrumental in mitigating some of the adverse effects? And, lastly, what are some of the non-income-related forms of social disparity that affect mobility and the achievement of more socially inclusive outcomes?

Growing disillusionment with economic policy making

If technology-intensive growth and innovation with its accompanying challenges of labor displacement and other forms of disruption are among the great trends in contemporary capitalism, the other surely must be the rising levels of socioeconomic disparity across many of the world's advanced economies. Echoing arguments made in his widely read book, *Globalization and Its Discontents* (2002), economist Joseph Stiglitz recently highlighted how what used to be a pervasive discontent with the presumed benefits of increased global economic integration through the multilateral trading system in the developing world has changed to include many in the advanced economies today (*Straits Times*, August, 2016). It has become commonplace to hear of the disillusionment with the promises made by proponents of globalization, which have been countered so emphatically by neoliberals they tend to be of the sort that people are in fact better off – they just do not realize it.

Looking closer, however, the reasons for growing disillusionment seem to be well-founded. However, this disillusionment should also include a recognition that it is not just globalization that is behind rising inequality and the fact that the benefits of economic growth have not been more widely shared. Technological innovation and its role in helping economies create more value with less labor are a structural reality of today's advanced economies. It will likely gain momentum as the pace of automation quickens across a growing array of sectors and blue-collar and white-collar occupations alike, as noted previously. In addition, the changing nature of capital–labor relationships has, as also alluded to earlier, been another accelerating trend that has had significant impacts on the employment relationship, squeezing wages and benefits and generally making work significantly more precarious for a good many. Despite a recent uptick in wage growth in OECD (Organization for Economic Co-operation and Development) economies in the last two or three years, especially in the United States, the long-term trend has been one of stagnant or falling wages for over 20 years, in some cases, for many working-class households (*Economist*, 2015; International Labour Organization, 2016). This job growth, which for the last several years at least has been more robust in some of the larger of the world's advanced economies, still invites important questions as to the sources of employment creation and the stability of those jobs, either in the full-time or part-time nature of the work or in the wage and benefits structure. So, many of the things such as greater economic openness, technological advance, and business model innovations that are supposed to make today's economies richer, more productive, and generally healthier and more stable have not delivered many of their anticipated benefits, at least not in the ways some had hoped or expected.

It is increasingly difficult not to admit that these trends are central to rising discontent with the economic order, especially the way that economic institutions are being structured to reproduce and distribute the gains from growth. Under such circumstances, the pronounced move away from greater economic integration in several of the world's largest economies – including the United States, Great Britain, and possibly others in Europe in the years ahead – punctuated with populist political arguments about the need for greater economic nationalism, is a response to emerging imbalance in the way many economies are functioning. The same applies to a number of international agreements on trade such as the recent withdrawal by the United States from the Trans-Pacific Partnership (TPP), increasing skepticism also in the United States toward other long-standing agreements such as the North American Free Trade Agreement (NAFTA) and even on matters of crucial multilateral cooperation for realizing the goals of a global framework for tackling climate change under the recently concluded Paris Agreement. The financialization of many if not most advanced economies has continued despite the painful consequences of the global financial crisis of 2008–2009 and the costly bailouts given to banks and large corporations for decision making that contributed substantially to the crisis in the first place. All of this is calling into question in new ways the intelligence and presumed benefits of national economic policy making. If one of the conclusions we can draw from this is that an increasingly widespread disenchantment with the prevailing economic structure is beginning to set in, based in large measure on the distributional consequences of ever more significant numbers of people not advancing up the socioeconomic ladder, where must we look to assess its likely causes? And what might this suggest in terms of ways to remedy the situation?

Anglo-American market economies, particularly the United States, are seen as global leaders in an oft talked about trend of widening disparity. However, economies in Europe with traditionally stronger social welfare systems are also struggling with the same phenomenon. As complicated a topic as this is, the debate has also been a widely researched one, and many of the analyses point to at least two key factors. The first is fiscal policy that has helped reinforce the rate of growth of capital income in a sustained manner relative to the rate of growth of the economy as a whole, which has increased the returns to capital ownership (Piketty, 2013). The other is perhaps more of an American phenomenon, although not exclusively. That is the relatively lax environment surrounding corporate governance, especially the way executive/CEO compensation has been allowed to reach such extraordinary levels and often in a manner quite divorced from performance.[1] Surely other important factors are contributing to the accelerated polarization of incomes, but these two have had a profound impact on rising inequality across some of the world's largest and most advanced economies.

Social mobility and the middle class

There is ample evidence to support the proposition that most households in advanced economies today simply are not advancing. As noted, an increasing proportion of households in many advanced economies are experiencing sustained income stagnation or actual declines in real (inflation-adjusted) income for extended periods of close to 15 years, and in some cases, twice as long. In the United States for instance, those in the bottom 90% of the income distribution have experienced income stagnation for roughly 30 years, while the median income for full-time male workers is actually lower in real terms today than it was nearly 40 years ago (U.S. Bureau of the Census, 2015; Donovan et al., 2016). At the lowest ends of the distribution, real wages are comparable to their levels almost 50 years ago. As previously alluded to, however, these kinds of stalled social mobility outcomes for large segments of the population are by no means unique to the United States. A number of other economies in the industrialized world, including ones with stronger social safety nets, have been seeing similar results, albeit with less extreme effects.

Recent work carried out by the McKinsey Global Institute (2016b), covering 25 OECD countries, takes a longitudinal perspective to the study of income trends. The central findings make comparisons between time periods but concentrate on the 2005–2014 period and show that across all of these countries, some 65–70% of households were in income segments that have experienced flat or declining incomes in 2014 compared to 2005. It is estimated this covers approximately 540 million people. When contrasted with different time periods such as 1993–2005, the study notes differences that are quite stark. In this latter period, the report finds that a mere 2% of households saw such stagnant or declining incomes. An important consideration in the interpretation of this analysis, however, must be the sensitivity of outcomes to the choice of time periods themselves. For instance, the mid- to late 1990s extending to approximately 2002 was a period of abnormally rapid growth across North America and many parts of Europe due to the Internet boom and accompanying dot.com revolution, as well as significant property price appreciation, which helped feed dramatic household consumption in many countries (Stiglitz, 2003). In Eastern Europe, economic growth began to pick up considerably in the late 1990s, following several years of shoddy privatization programs and other efforts directed at transforming the economic institutions of socialism (Amsden, 1994). This was principally related to new foreign investment into moribund formerly state-run sectors, as well as the rather low starting point from which economic growth was occurring. Earlier time periods spanning the 1970s and 1980s would likely produce less dramatic comparisons as those between 2005 and 2014, given that this latter included the global financial crisis.

Perhaps the most important part of the study, however, rests with the assertion that the scale of the income stagnation or declines would have been considerably more negative if it had not been for how taxes and transfers provided a crucial buffer against these relative losses of market income. In other words, either reduced taxation or increases in benefits and other income supports were crucial aspects of government policy that helped keep some of these income groups from experiencing even more starkly negative reductions in income. Although macroeconomic forces, particularly the global recession following the financial crisis, weighed heavily among the factors contributing to these wage outcomes, other variables were of great significance, revealing important differences among countries. Notable factors include demographic changes, particularly in Europe, characterized by smaller households with fewer working-age adults; labor market shifts that have seen declining shares of total output going to labor and weak demand for lower-skilled labor in particular; and, finally, low levels of capital income held by most households in these stagnating or declining income segments. Interestingly, in countries where levels of unionization were stronger, such as in Sweden and to a lesser extent France, the impact of adverse labor market shifts was less severe.

It should therefore not be surprising that, in this context of sustained depressed household incomes across many of today's advanced economies, people are adopting increasingly negative attitudes about the future. The McKinsey research presented results from survey work that showed pessimism to be widespread and on the rise about future prospects ranging from personal economic progress to the life chances of future generations, as well as negative views toward global trade being responsible for domestic job loss and unfair competition. In addition, this skepticism is spilling into the social realm, with greater numbers of people in these stagnant or declining income segments expressing unfavorable attitudes regarding how cultural identity and social cohesion are being disrupted through increased immigration. Given these economic trends, it has been asserted that predicting the rise of populist and economic nationalist thinking across many of these advanced economies, as seen through Brexit and the election of Donald Trump as president in the United States, should have been possible and should not be regarded as surprising by anyone. This is a further manifestation of globalization's new discontents.

If the importance of taxes and transfers were the single most important factor in buffering vulnerable populations against even more welfare-compromising outcomes, the sustainability of these public sector income supports is crucial, and all the more so if growth is likely to continue benefitting a smaller share of the population. Promoting more broad-based growth is thus essential to reestablishing social mobility and in turn confidence in public institutions and in economic policy making, something that appears to be in danger of being eroded considerably if current trends persist unchecked. Reviving growth prospects through economic policy must first embrace technological change and, second, recognize the fact that, despite the near-term potential for a retrenchment, globalization is an inexorable trend and one that is becoming increasingly digitized. Considering an economy like the United States, which has historically never been that dependent on foreign trade for economic growth as a percentage of its GNP (Kravis, 1970), fewer than 1% of U.S. companies today export anything. As the United States is the outright global leader in creating digital content, it becomes easier to see how the 2% growth rate could quite realistically be on the order of 3% or even 3.5% if more incentives were given to digitizing business processes and helping small and medium-size enterprises put their products and services online. This is a point made by the McKinsey Global

Institute's Jonathan Woetzel, speaking about the "need to get on the right side of global trends" in order to restore economic growth that has better chances to improve income prospects for the large numbers of people who have been living with incomes that are not keeping up with cost-of-living increases. Although it is not immediately clear how this would translate to income gains for disadvantaged workers or business owners, it is likely that enabling SMEs to more actively participate and directly benefit from global economic activity and interconnectedness will expand the array of business and income opportunities they face. As national (extraregional) and international collaborations are on the rise in many if not most advanced economies, creating new networked approaches to growth through collaborative innovation, the link between digitization, exporting, and overall business expansion should be regarded as an interconnected set of policy priorities for cities in particular, which will often have a firmer grasp on the SMEs in their jurisdictions.

Persistent underinvesting in housing and infrastructure has also been an important factor in the social and economic decline of many cities in OECD countries. This has had negative consequences in other ways, such as forcing people to live farther away from new job centers, creating new difficulties in maintaining city schools and making them less attractive and effective, and giving momentum to an out-migration of companies and wealthier households, often reinforcing a cycle of shrinking tax bases and further disinvestment (Dewar and Thomas, 2012). Overcoming a growing infrastructure deficit, however, is certainly not just an economic or technical matter and is very much about the politics of public finance.

Periods of low economic growth such as has been the case in recent years, particularly across much of Europe, places strain on public resources and makes it more difficult to find political acceptance for large-scale infrastructure spending even if such new investments are a significant employment generator. The current political environment in the United States, which is badly in need of major infrastructure investment across many metropolitan regions, is pitting local and state governments from different jurisdictions against a federal government and a new administration that has infrastructure spending supposedly among its priorities but that faces many competing claims on resources and fractious political interests. The often fragmented nature of a democratic capitalist system is often held up as a reason for why stronger or more unitary states such as some of those in Asia, like China, Taiwan, and Singapore or even the Gulf States, are increasingly regarded as infrastructure leaders and developing world-class highways, rail systems, bridges and tunnels, and airports. It is in fact to some of the far-reaching implications of economic development in China that the focus shifts.

Global pressures from the economic rise of China

For many years since economic reforms began in China in 1978, the concept of gradualism was most appropriate to describe the pace and character of China's way of transforming its economy. Although still nothing like the "shock therapy" model attempted in the former Soviet Union and much of Eastern Europe during the early and mid-1990s with the most dubious results, the momentum behind China's reforms has been magnified significantly by the country's sustained economic development. Even though the reform process remains an ongoing transformation that often proceeds in fits and starts, the words that better describe economic change in China today are "speed" and "scale," according to Professor Tan Kong Yam of the Lee Kuan Yew School of Public Policy's Asia Competitiveness Institute. Although China's real GDP growth rates have been slowing over the last five years, in the vicinity of 8% average annual growth between 2009 and 2015, as opposed to roughly 10% for the preceding years extending back to 2000 (IMF, 2016), Professor Tan stresses that the pace of growth, combined with the scale effects, has enabled the Chinese economy to surpass other large economies ever more rapidly. This has dramatically expanded its resource base and consumer market, only increasing the possibilities for further transformation and growth. The extent of China's economic development is, of course, felt all around the world with important implications for global growth, including new pressures on advanced economies to manage the globalization and trade consequences of China's ascendancy.

Several important factors come into play. The first involves a rising middle class in China that is significantly adding to global wealth creation, as well as absorbing considerable resources from outside China to serve a long anticipated consumer revolution. This comes with the possibility of moving more production, marketing, and businesses services work closer to this expanding market and possibly away from slower growing markets in Europe and elsewhere. This is something that could compound already slow job creation in these markets. Another involves China's harnessing its sizable science and technology research establishment, which has been undergoing substantial opening up over the last 25 years, to make a push into advanced industries. The result has been a progressive expansion of its innovative capabilities through a sustained increase in its research and development (R&D) activity. As this innovation drive makes the Chinese economy more competitive in advanced industries, this is likely to add to global trade-related tensions, which are significant across as well as within countries at present. Still another, rising numbers of educated workers in China, rising wages, and appreciation of the yuan are all forcing a rapid upgrading of its industrial structure.

Although China's sustained growth is serving to make significant improvements in the global poverty statistics and thus is contributing to more inclusive outcomes on an international scale, there are certainly more troublesome prospects in the way that other economies are likely to encounter increasing trade-related pressures. This will be felt in a more competitive environment for private investment, tightening supplies of skilled labor, and a continuation of a trend of declining shares of national income going to medium and low-skilled labor, which will likely increase the need for higher levels of public expenditure on income support and especially worker retraining programs. As all three of these processes deepen and become more mature in the Chinese economy, their impact will be felt quite significantly on the already burdened middle class in many OECD countries. Within China, one of the major issues the economy will have to contend with is the supply-side bottlenecks that are becoming more acute as regards demand for housing, schools, other basic infrastructure and sociocultural amenities, in order to accommodate the inward flow of 10–15 million people into Chinese cities each year. Notwithstanding the comments made previously about the relative effectiveness of the Chinese state being able to deliver on infrastructure, this constitutes some of the double-edged domestic characteristics of the scale of Chinese growth because this kind of rural-to-urban migration will strain any economy.

Note

1 For a more thorough account of how executive boards are structured and operate in the formulation of executive compensation in particular, see Bebchuck and Fried (2004) and Stiglitz (2003, 2013: chapter 2).

4   Infrastructure for the future

OBJECTIVE

In a field that has long been characterized by a "tyranny of the experts," namely engineers and planners, what are some of the ways this orthodoxy is being challenged? Can infrastructure be designed to really reflect the diversity of wants and needs within today's communities? In what ways are new technologies able to improve the planning, operation, and governance of existing and future infrastructure systems? Finally, how can ordinary people be involved in not just the conversation about infrastructure but the planning and design of it as well?

The word "infrastructure" is of relatively recent origin, first appearing in French in the late 19th century. It comes from a combination of the Latin prefix "infra," which means "below" and "structure," which would suggest that it refers to the underpinnings of an operating system. However, the definition of the word has evolved. A study by the U.S. National Academy of Sciences in 1987 suggested that the meaning of the word "infrastructure" should include not only conventional public works facilities but also:

> the operating procedures, management practices, and development policies that interact together with societal demand and the physical world to facilitate the transport of people and goods, provision of water for drinking and a variety of other uses, safe disposal of society's waste products, provision of energy where it is needed, and transmission of information within and between communities.
>
> (*Infrastructure for the 21st Century*, 1987)

It is this broader definition that is used here. The importance of infrastructure was, of course, recognized long before it became the subject of formal study. As early as 4000 BCE, societies built canals, irrigation systems, and roads, sometimes paved, to facilitate transportation. However, it was not until the 19th century that there was a quantum leap in the provision of infrastructure. The 19th century saw extraordinary advances in transportation and connectivity through steam power, the building of railways, the telegraph and telephone, the first electrical systems, as well as water treatment and sewerage systems. These systems were greatly expanded and improved upon in the first half of the 20th century, evolving into far more robust networks of mass transit, power grids, and telecommunications systems. By the close of the 20th century, there had been a sea change in the way people and organizations communicate and conduct business through the development and extraordinary expansion of the Internet. These different systems and networks are now more interconnected than ever, also complicating issues of management and maintenance in order to ensure system reliability.

Economists began to formally study infrastructure development and its impact on economies. This impact is broadly twofold. First, it was recognized, especially after the work of John Maynard Keynes in the 1930s, that investments in infrastructure can boost aggregate demand through multiplier effects, which is why it has since often been used as a demand management tool. Second, infrastructure also strengthens the supply side of an economy by increasing or improving productive capacity. In the session on Infrastructure, the chairperson Cheong Koon Hean, CEO of Singapore's Housing and Development Board (HDB), sketched out some basic ideas to frame some big picture issues. First, there is the issue of dealing with existing infrastructure. This has to be rigorously maintained; otherwise widespread service disruption can be the result if maintenance is not carried out properly. At the same time, however, infrastructure must cater to new demands and be as future-ready as possible. Second, the emergence of new information and communication technologies puts pressure on cities to modernize their current systems in order to remain competitive. Cities that do not plan up front and embrace new technologies would find it hard to cope with the demands of rapid urbanization, while those that do are likely to reap the benefits of increased economic growth and be better able to serve their citizens more effectively. Other than technology, there is also a need to adopt or build appropriate business models for infrastructure and apply them to the delivery of public services, particularly given how infrastructure requires substantial resources, which is a concern for governments facing budget constraints. So there is a need to explore innovative approaches to infrastructure financing. But infrastructure is not only about hardware. At the end of the day, it must serve citizens, which in turn raises issues such as engaging citizens in planning infrastructure that meets their needs, achieving greater social equity, and ensuring access.

Unmet needs

It is difficult to talk about infrastructure in today's economies without grappling with the large unmet demand for it. As the World Bank notes, many people in developing countries face serious shortfalls as regards reliable and affordable infrastructure. The resulting economic and social costs are enormous. Over 1.3 billion people, almost 20% of the world's population, still do not have electricity. Approximately 770 million people worldwide lack access to clean water, and 2.5 billion do not have adequate sanitation. This infrastructure deficit in developing economies is estimated at more than US$1 trillion a year.[1] More advanced economies are by no means free from a concern about the damaging effects related to sustained infrastructure deficits. In its recent report on the state of basic infrastructure in the United States, the American Society of Civil Engineers (ASCE, 2016) assigned a D+ rating for the country's roads, bridges, waterways, and airports. It estimated the funding gap to be more than $3.3 trillion between 2016 and 2025. It cautioned that a failure to bridge this gap would take a heavy toll in terms of higher costs for business, lower productivity, longer travel times, more expensive goods and services for households, and lower total output across the economy. In other words, it would likely have a significant dampening effect on economic growth.

Other advanced economies in Europe and elsewhere also face significant infrastructure shortfalls. The McKinsey Global Institute (2016) points out that infrastructure investment has actually declined as a share of GDP in 11 of the G20 economies since the global financial crisis of 2008. It estimates that from 2016 through 2030, the world needs to invest about 3.8% of GDP, or an average of $3.3 trillion a year, on infrastructure just to keep up with expected growth. Emerging economies account for some 60% of that need, but if the current trajectory of underinvestment continues, the world will fall short by roughly $350 billion a year.

Future-ready infrastructure

Asserting that there are three ways to address the massive unmet infrastructure needs, Dr. Peter Edwards, director of Singapore's ETH Centre (of the Eidgenössische Technische Hochschule in Zurich, also known as the Swiss Federal Institute of Technology), cited reducing demand, building new assets, and optimizing existing assets as central to this objective. The emergence of new technologies present important opportunities to achieve each of these goals to modernize infrastructure systems in innovative ways and indeed to change the dominant assumption about what kinds of infrastructure are needed for the future.

For large systems for water, transport, and energy, for instance, he mentions how contemporary thinking has essentially developed outside the era of the Internet. "The whole philosophy, the paradigm and the management of these assets, haven't really embraced Internet thinking," he said. Many infrastructure systems have become increasingly massive and centralized. He cited the newly planned Hinkley Point nuclear power station in England, where the construction costs, as well as those for decommissioning many years from now, will be very significant. These types of large centralized systems have three implications, according to Dr. Edwards. First, they involve very heavy investments as well as long planning horizons and life spans, which means returns on investment are also earned over long periods. This leads to an overdesign tendency on the part of engineers, sometimes massive overdesign, in order to have reserve capacity because "you cannot afford to fail." Second, they also tend to have low resilience, especially in the face of unforeseen circumstances or events. Although such systems are designed to be as robust as possible, they are vulnerable to failure, and when they fail, the results can be quite devastating. The example of Fukushima is a case in point.[2] Third, large centralized systems also promote overconsumption of resources. For example, massive roads lead to increased usage, more travel, and longer travel times. Big cities tend to appropriate large hinterlands to produce water, with little thought given to how to save it. In short, the issue is becoming one of how such systems may reduce incentives for people to generate less waste, recycle more, or just generally adopt more resource-rational behavior.

Can infrastructure planning in the age of the Internet help reduce spatial distortions and even serve to slow rapid levels of urbanization, including the formation of mega cities? Infrastructure has always drawn people into big cities. In the Internet era, however, people are easily networked; societies can be connected despite being geographically dispersed. Increasingly significant aspects of social interaction occur through social media. Economies are also highly networked through data-powered exchanges and various other mobile communications technologies. Explaining how there is "an ineluctable logic of the Internet," Dr. Edwards implies that decentralization is often a better option. "If you are connected with everyone else, there are all sorts of ways of doing business." This in turn has profound implications for the future of infrastructure. For instance, since infrastructure has traditionally been overdesigned, there is much that can be done with reserve capacity. Wi-fi–based sensors and diagnostic tools can help city and infrastructure managers to better understand the capacity of bridges and roads so that they do not have to be replaced prematurely. Surveys in the United States and Europe show that 80% of the bridges need to be replaced. Dr. Edwards asks how do we know this for sure? In his view, modern wi-fi sensor technology has the potential to release a lot of that capacity.

It is worth noting that this question about advances in communications technology and enhanced connectivity being a factor that can slow urbanization, or even lead to the decline of cities, has a long history among urban scholars. This has ranged from Frank Lloyd Wright's vision about a deconcentrated metropolis, albeit in a pre-Internet world, that he called "Broadacre City" in his book *The Disappearing City* (1932) to more recent notions of decentralized cities merging into new urban forms with the transformation of the suburb, enabled by advances in technology and communication, into what Fishman (1987) has called the "technoburb." As the debate continues today, there is increasing recognition that the Internet and communications advances are not yet having the kind of impact that would support a view that cities are declining in size or in economic significance. Where cities are shrinking, as in parts of the United States and Europe, this appears to be more a function of long-term shifts in the economic base of cities or broader demographic trends than it does about a movement against urbanization trends powered by the Internet and advanced communications technologies.[3]

In the future, Dr. Edwards suggested, there will likely be more of a mix of centralized and decentralized infrastructure systems. Some of this is already evident, for example, in privately generated solar energy feeding into power grids and the emergence of "autonomous buildings" that capture, process, and manage their own water, which could potentially even be added to city or national water systems. Greater use of information and communication technologies (ICT) could also make resource use more efficient and promote greater control over processes and resource use. Autonomous, smart transport systems that use sensors and big data carry the promise of enabling more effective use of road systems. The use of ICT in infrastructure could also lower capital costs and provide greater flexibility. Such systems are also likely to be more resilient, noting that "a much more networked infrastructure with many more small providers leads to more resilience."

The question of whether more decentralized infrastructure systems could in fact help curb the growth of very large urban areas, has enormous implications especially for Asia, where it is estimated that by 2050, 1.3 billion more people will be living in cities than is currently the case today. The current consensus is that those future cities will be high-density areas, supported by centralized infrastructure, such as large power plants, waste treatment facilities, road networks, and water systems. However, the logic of the Internet means that this need not be how things will develop. Asserting how he believes there will be a much greater diversity of forms of infrastructure with small decentralized systems, coupled with large centralized systems, Dr. Edwards indicated that the pattern might vary geographically according to circumstances and levels of development. This poses a challenge for large utilities, as it threatens returns on investment and their basic business models. More decentralized forms of infrastructure are already a reality in parts of the developed world, as evidenced by the emergence of large markets for small-scale water processing and electricity generating systems. The logic and power of the Internet will advance and make more clear the benefits of decentralization, and this will "begin to infiltrate into the thinking about infrastructure, we will see a transformation in how we relate to and construct our infrastructure."

"Whole system" approaches

With a focus on some of the immediate challenges facing the region and the issues that must be considered when planning urban infrastructure, Scott Dunn, vice president for Southeast Asia at AECOM, said a key challenge is to find the balance between building new infrastructure and rejuvenating aging infrastructure, a point raised by Cheong Koon Hean, the HDB chairperson, at the outset. An important consideration here is the need to prioritize projects to deal with immediate, pressing issues. For instance, in Australia where 85% of the population lives in coastal areas, the problem of massive flooding drove the agenda to provide for flood mitigation systems to protect communities and property assets. Metropolitan areas in Southeast Asia such as Jakarta, Manila, and Ho Chi Minh City face similar challenges.

Infrastructure must also be designed and built to be convenient for people. For instance, when it comes to providing mobility for both people and goods, urban rail systems are expanding rapidly in many major cities. But providing mobility is more than the core rail network; it is also about planning around how people move through a city and connect with the community. Scott Dunn mentions how "careful consideration needs to be given to the first and last kilometre of peoples' journeys," which calls for an integrated approach involving many stakeholders. Such an integrated approach requires thinking about "whole systems" when it comes to providing facilities for communities. He cites the ways in which mixed-use developments which integrate residential, commercial, retail, and transportation facilities, have the potential to create more jobs closer to where people live and can be at the same time well connected with the wider city. A successful case in point, according to Scott Dunn, is Fort Bonifacio in Manila, a former military base about 11 kilometers from the city center, which has been transformed into a mini city. The heart of it is centered around Bonifacio High Street, which comprises a mix of high-tech offices, residential buildings, retail outlets, pedestrian-friendly roads and walkways, as well as landscaped areas and parks. Designed as a grid, it is easy to navigate and is well connected with the rest of Manila. Similar developments have come up in Chengdu, Ningbo, and Shanghai, other cities in China, as well as in Ho Chi Minh City. In Singapore, where the central business district is still quite dominated by office towers, there has been a progressive move toward mixed-use development featuring residential, retail, and leisure facilities. The experience with mixed-use developments in most advanced economies is not new. Their purported claims of accommodating mixed-income residents, increased density, diversity, provision of affordable housing, and improved employment trends are, on the whole, quite varied. The success of mixed-use developments often depends upon the relative strength and bargaining power of local government versus property developers, buy-in from employers, and local community dynamics.[4]

Having served on the Future City Subcommittee of the Government of Singapore's Committee on the Future Economy (CFE), which released its report in February 2017, Scott Dunn discussed some of the key opportunities that Singapore could pursue in the area of urban infrastructure. The first relates to creating the data infrastructure for a digital world. Drawing a parallel to how transshipment works, where at the Port of Singapore, approximately 95% of containers that dock in Singapore are routed to other destinations, the question is, "How do you do the same thing with the digital infrastructure?" – in other words, shaping an ecosystem that allows Singapore and other economies in the region to capitalize on managing and harnessing data and providing analytics to create value. This cannot be done without a strong set of steps taken to ensure a secure environment. Safety and security are critical across all infrastructure; particularly as "smart," Internet-connected infrastructure expands, there is a growing need to protect against threats. Therefore, the need to provide robust cybersecurity to protect critical urban infrastructure is of particular importance.

Second, new challenges for infrastructure and management stemming from the rise of e-commerce are asserting themselves. Currently, in Singapore about 30% of peak traffic results from the movement of goods around the island. As e-commerce continues to expand, more congestion in the road network is sure to follow. The options being examined include creating regional distribution centers connected to port and airport facilities; enabling consolidated deliveries for last-kilometer connections; using locker systems or parcel transportation systems that might be automated through rail; and deploying drones for delivery, including creating dedicated corridors for drones.

Third, building more sustainability and resilience around core infrastructure assets is another priority of the CFE. In energy, the challenge is to diversify sources of energy away from gas to include solar, wind, hydro, and other forms of energy. On the demand side, an aim is to create "smart grids" and "smart buildings" that can help reduce demand during high-cost peak periods. In the area of water, resilience could be enhanced through more rainwater harvesting and deploying new desalination technologies. Food security is another area of focus for the CFE. Singapore imports more than 90% of its food, and this could be reduced by harnessing innovations in vertical farming and improving yields and nutritional properties in locally produced foods such as eggs, vegetables, and seafood. In the end, building resilience in infrastructure, according to Scott Dunn, is about being adaptable and flexible and using innovation to seize new opportunities.

The case of long-range infrastructure planning and resilience in the UK

Presenting some of the work being undertaken in the UK under its National Infrastructure Commission (NIC), Brian Collins, professor of engineering policy at University College London, discussed how the country is developing a long-term strategy for infrastructure. The NIC's vision has three basic elements:

- First, it must be credible; otherwise its advice to government and to industry will not be heeded.
- Second, it must be forward-thinking and not backward-reacting. This means it must look at long-term priorities and ensure that any short-term actions or policies that it proposes are compatible with those priorities. It must also view infrastructure as a set of interdependent systems, not as a collection of silos. "Forward-looking" also means assuming an international approach, taking into account how international aspects of infrastructure work, particularly the changing structure and functioning of supply chains.
- Third, it must be an influential voice on both policy and strategy. This requires clear communication, cutting through the jargon that is so much a part of the vocabulary of experts in the field of infrastructure. It also means that the NIC must be independent of government or vested interests.

The theme of infrastructure resilience, in the context of balancing the new and the old, was again advanced as an important issue. While promoting innovation in infrastructure, including harnessing disruptive technologies, is certainly important, so is maintaining old or so-called legacy infrastructure systems. Citing how there is much political capital to be gained from delivering brand-new infrastructure projects, Brian Collins mentioned how maintaining existing systems may actually deliver a much more effective solution for society and for business. The NIC is doing a lot of research on the issue of infrastructure resilience. One key question in this area is how to move from preventing failure to ensuring functionality. This involves thinking not only about the physical parameters of infrastructure but also about whether critical services and functions can be provided in some other ways, at least temporarily, when large system operations are put under stress. Creating this "bounce-back ability," especially for legacy infrastructure, is an important aspect of resilience. Integrating the old with the new, driving innovation while at the same time protecting effective existing systems, is important to overall system resilience. As he stated, "We mustn't forget that everything we do in infrastructure, in cities in particular, has to integrate with legacy in some appropriate way." The design of infrastructure must focus on performance rather than just on systems and assets, with resilience being explicitly valued and built into business models. This requires buy-in of all those involved with infrastructure projects, from the project owners to the financiers and insurers. Finally, the integration of systems thinking and principles of resilience into engineering education will be an important factor in conceptualizing better infrastructure systems. Too often the interdependence of different infrastructure assets is overlooked with insufficient holistic thinking about what constitutes robust and resilient systems.

Resilience and interdependence

During the massive floods in Jakarta in February 2015, the local authorities decided to shut down the electricity in the city to protect residents from electrocution. As a result, the power supply to the water pumps in the city was also shut off, leaving the city unable to pump storm water out of the city. As more rains came, this led to even more severe flooding, which lasted for many days.

Between December 2013 and February 2014, England experienced an unusual succession of severe storms, which led to widespread floods across the southeast of the country. The flooding of the power station that served Gatwick airport led to flights being canceled. Many power lines were damaged, and roads blocked by fallen trees and debris rendered parts of the road and rail networks dysfunctional.

Hurricane Sandy, which hit the East Coast of the United States and New York on October 22, 2012, was the worst natural disaster in the city's history, destroyed thousands of homes, and led to 43 deaths. Some 2 million people lost power. These electricity disruptions affected the functioning of a range of other sectors, while subway, bus, and commuter rail services had to be suspended. Telecommunications networks also went down, and even the health care system was hit with some 6,500 patients, including many in intensive care, needing to be evacuated from hospitals and nursing homes.[5]

As alluded to by Brian Collins, infrastructure facilities and the experts who plan them have traditionally tended to operate in silos. Electricity is managed by power companies, water is provided by water utilities, railways are run by railway companies. Telecommunications and Internet service providers, however, are typically provided by multiple vendors. The reason for such single-focused corporate structures is generally thought to be the high fixed capital costs and low margins on service provision, making cost recovery on capital investment a long-term prospect. However, as the preceding examples illustrate, the failure of one critical piece of infrastructure can have devastating and disruptive effects on broader systems. Sometimes, multiple infrastructure facilities are mutually dependent. Take the case of a power plant that runs on coal, where the coal is transported to the plant via trains, which in turn need power from the plant in order to operate. A failure in one of these facilities can affect the others.

There are many types of interdependency across systems and facilities. One is physical interdependence, where one facility needs material inputs from another in order to function properly. Another is geographic interdependency. A natural disaster affecting a particular geographical area – severe flooding, for example – can knock out different types of infrastructure facilities in that area. There are also cyber-interdependencies. Advances in sensor, network, and software technologies, as well as data analytics, have led to many infrastructure systems being monitored and maintained with the help of ICT. Problems within ICT networks can in turn lead to disruptions in other infrastructure systems. Researchers also point to a fourth interdependency, which they term logical interdependency. The state of each infrastructure depends on the state of the other via a mechanism that is neither physical, nor geographic, nor cyber related but that occurs as a result of human decisions (Rinaldi et al., 2001). What is needed therefore is a "system of systems approach" to managing infrastructure, where interdependencies are identified and plans put in place to ensure, as far as possible, that disruptions in one area do not compromise the functioning of others.[6]

Infrastructure as a shared vision

Continuing with the idea of a broadening-out of stakeholder groups in the development of infrastructure systems, Professor Nick Tyler of University

College London focused on the idea of infrastructure as a shared vision, involving local governments, professionals, as well as communities. As alluded to previously, professionals such as architects, engineers, and planners have traditionally dominated the process of determining the rationale and the end goals of infrastructure facilities, including their design and construction. So, on balance, the process has always been weighted in favor of the professionals, and people and the communities of which they are a part often tend to feel left out. An alternative approach is to give a higher weighting to community needs, even to the extent of giving relatively less influence to the professionals. The key is based in communicative processes aimed at building mutual understanding between professionals and people in which professionals communicate their knowledge in a way that people can understand. Out of that evolves what Dr. Tyler described as "a high-level, far-reaching vision" of transformation – not of the type that a politician may articulate as an election promise but rather a much larger-scale vision.

A critical part of the conversation between professionals and people is about determining what society wants: talking with the community to work out what they actually want and what they need and then translating "that into something which is meaningful," according to Nick Tyler. Trade-offs must be considered in this process. Is society prepared to accept what the changes will involve or whether it is willing to forgo some of its needs? There are always trade-offs in the building of infrastructure, especially given financial constraints. When local budgets are allocated to big projects that have major implications for national interconnectedness, such as highways, ports, or airports, this will reduce the resources available for infrastructure that is critical for local communities, such as housing, public schools, and health care facilities. Only with community involvement can such trade-offs be identified and addressed. Thus, the process of finding out what society wants and understanding what it really means and involves is important, according to Nick Tyler, "because it establishes an accepted and shared vision, not just one that somebody has proposed. It also starts a conversation on how the city is going to progress." It is important to recognize some of the scholarly critiques of community participation and what is often referred to as "communicative rationality" emanating from planning circles and broader social theory. Some of the presumed merits tend to be rather romanticized in that such participatory and communication-based approaches are, at least in theory, predicated on a Habermasian "ideal speech" setting. Many of these community-centered, multistakeholder, and collaborative planning modes, however laudable, tend to minimize the significance of differential power relationships and some of the underlying discriminatory biases that exist in such contexts that in turn can distort the end result. The implication being that good or well-intentioned processes do not always yield good outcomes or at least ones that are truly reflective of the wants and needs of a community.[7]

Taking the case of Medellin, Colombia, as a shared vision for urban renewal being turned into reality, transformative change has gradually taken root. As the second largest city in Colombia with a population of 2.5 million, it was known in the late 1980s and early 1990s as the murder capital of the world, dominated by violent crime and drug cartels. Entire neighborhoods were off-limits even to law enforcement officials, and children in poorer neighborhoods were afraid to attend school. Since then, massive investments in infrastructure, coupled with more effective policing and forward-looking social policies, have progressively reversed the city's catastrophic situation. New investment in transportation systems, green spaces, and a range of community services and cultural assets has made Medellin a city that is not only safe – the murder rate fell more than 80% between 1991 and 2007 – but that offers a quality of life that ranked among the highest in Latin America. In 2013, Medellin was voted the world's most innovative city in an online poll conducted by the Urban Land Institute, which compiled a list of 200 cities based on eight criteria ranging from culture and livability to education and infrastructure. In 2016, Medellin was awarded the Lee Kuan Yew World City Prize by the Singapore government, beating 38 other cities in contention that year.

The key point underscored by Nick Tyler in speaking about Medellin is that citizen participation in community and municipal decision making played a critical role in the city's transformation. Frequent meetings between city officials and community leaders helped ensure that the investments made and services provided helped make a real difference to peoples' lives. For example, the authorities built fountains for recreation near water projects. Spaces around infrastructure facilities that were otherwise empty or fenced off were converted into centers for the arts and education. This illustrates that even relatively small interventions can have a big impact on the quality of life, all of which helps to provide momentum to sustain broader social and economic reforms and initiatives. There were bigger changes as well, such as an integrated transport system that extended into the mountains around Medellin so that rural producers could more easily sell their farm produce in the city. Even the primary education curriculum was changed to encourage children to learn about local environmental issues.

People-centric design

Planning to accommodate the needs of future generations will be an important success factor for cities going forward. A city is not something static that is designed and then stopped; rather, cities are about evolution. The next generation will require different things from what the city is now, and that will be determined by the next generation. Planning and design in the city must leave open options for future generations to be able to meet their own needs.

The adoption of "smart" features in infrastructure systems must also be considered in terms of what people want and need. Asserting how it is not only about technology but also about people, Nick Tyler advances that the technology has to be simple, multiscale, available to everybody, and relevant to the way people live their lives and interact in the city. Regarding autonomous vehicles for example, even though they may be technologically feasible or close to it, the question that must be asked is in what ways they are likely to benefit people? A more thorough consideration of what problems autonomous vehicles will really solve is necessary. And are they the best way of solving those problems for people in cities? Once answers to these questions are known, then working out how autonomous vehicles can be made into part of the best solution can be undertaken. This should be done first, before going too far down the road of implementation.

Notes

1 See the data and information presented by the World Bank and its Global Infrastructure Facility, December 2016, at www.worldbank.org/en/programs/global-Infrastructure-facility
2 Nuclear reactors in Fukishima, Japan, were badly damaged following the tsunami of March 2011, leading to dangerous levels of radioactivity around the area, which persisted for years.
3 For thoughtful consideration of these and related issues, see Castells (1989) and Glaeser (2011).
4 For some critical perspective on mixed-use developments from a broad international perspective, see Wardner (2014). For a more industry-focused review of the developments and trends, see Rabianski and Clements (2007).
5 For more details on the impact of Hurricane Sandy on New York City and the metropolitan region, see the report by the New York City Mayor's Office, "Sandy and Its Impacts" (Government of New York City, n.d.) at www.nyc.gov/html/sirr/downloads/pdf/final_report/Ch_1_SandyImpacts_FINAL_singles.pdf
6 This notion of pursuing a better understanding of interdependency in infrastructure planning and operations is in line with the "whole systems" approach advanced by Scott Dunn and previously mentioned, in that it stresses a multisystem, multiactor way of thinking in order to deliver better performance from existing and planned infrastructure investments.
7 For a view of a procommunicative and collaborative planning agenda, see Healey (1992, 1997), and for a critique from an urban social justice standpoint, see Fainstein (2010).

5 The role of government in the future of the economy

OBJECTIVE

Given some of the great trends in the world today such as the future of work in an era of rapid technological advance, rising socioeconomic disparity, the strains of globalization, and the rise of nationalist economic thinking, how can the economic role of government be recast to be a positive force for broad-based growth? What levels of government can meaningfully address some of today's most pressing issues? What role must regional and city governments play? This chapter covers some important new ways of envisaging the conventional role of government in economic policy making and in addressing some key social issues.

Government's role in grappling with rising inequality

Although much has been made already of the problems stemming from rising – some might say exploding – income inequality in the advanced economies today, what can governments do to slow down this trend or otherwise better mitigate some of the consequences? This was the focus of the intervention of Professor Robert Wade of the London School of Economics, in which he first emphasized the magnitude of the problem, particularly in Anglo-American–style market economies. He noted that data from the United Nations Conference on Trade and Development (UNCTAD) has shown a pronounced shift in the share of global income that has gone to the capital share. The data shows that the labor share of global income has fallen from 62% in 1980 to 54% by 2011, which is a significant welfare-compromising trend. This corresponds with substantial financialization of many advanced economies, something that was given considerable momentum through the deregulation of the financial services industry during this same period. Currently, the top 1% of the population in the United States controls roughly 20% of national income, Robert Wade asks what might happen if this rises to one-third or even to half of the total wealth generated in the economy, and why should we care about this as a social problem? Citing how health and social problems such as crime and declining secondary school completion rates have become highly correlated with rising income inequality (Wilkinson and Pickett, 2009), one can begin to see real evidence for social decay linked to steady income polarization. Similar conclusions by Princeton University economists Anne Case and Angus Deaton have illustrated how life expectancy among particular segments of the white American population has been on the decline (Case and Deaton, 2017), including rising suicide rates, and have shown these outcomes to be linked to rising socioeconomic disparities.

As previously mentioned, the importance of taxes and transfers has helped in making a bad situation regarding the stagnation or declining incomes for many households in OECD economies over much of the last 20 years from being even worse. How much corrective or redistributive action can be accomplished through the mechanism of taxes and transfers is largely a political economy question since it runs into rather entrenched positions on the left and the right in those countries where income inequality is most serious. Contemplating other measures that can minimize inequality or at least slow its rate of growth will be important for the future. Given the sustained declines in the shares of national income going to labor in most advanced economies, with the exception of some of the Nordic countries where unionization is stronger and tripartite approaches to economic organization are more tested, some have argued for trying to help a wider segment of the population gain access to capital income than is currently the case.

While working class and poorer households are far more dependent on wage income, the wealthy and super wealthy have a much smaller share of their income accounted for by wages. In the United States, as presented by Stiglitz (2013: chapter 3), fewer than 7% of households earning less than $100,000 receive any capital gains, where it amounts to roughly 1.4% of income, whereas the top 1% of the income distribution derives 57% of income from capital gains and a further 16% from dividend income. A disproportionate access to capital income by wealthier segments of the population, however, is only part of the story that has fueled such growth in inequality in the United States. A key part involves the highly advantageous tax treatment of capital income in the United States for much of the last 16 years, which has seen this 73% share of income for the super wealthy (57% from capital gains and 16% from dividends) taxed at an astonishingly low rate of 15%. Since 2013, this rate has increased to 20%, with an additional 3.8% to help fund the Affordable Care Act, which is now under serious threat of being undermined by the current administration. Nevertheless, this has amounted to a very substantial transfer of wealth from the middle of the income distribution to the very wealthy and is further felt in billions of dollars in federal government revenue that has been forgone.[1] Considering that access to capital income is one of the primary drivers of income growth for the wealthier populations in advanced economies, it would seem a logical solution to try to help expand access to those portions of the population that have little of it. The problem is that the path to doing so is not altogether clear or proven.

Further thoughts on addressing the imbalance in access to capital income

The issue of access to capital income is fundamental to trends of rising disparity. As the French economist Thomas Piketty (2013) demonstrated in his influential book, *Capital in the 21st Century*, through analysis of long-term historical trends, the average rate of return (growth rate) to capital ownership has been greater over the long run than the returns to either wage income or the growth rate of national economies as a whole (something that he refers to quite simply in the inequality as "$r > g$," where r stands for the average annual rate of return on capital as a percentage of its total value – which includes everything from profits and dividends to interest and rents – and g stands for the growth rate of the economy as a whole, total output). His basic point is that, if the growth rate on capital ownership persists in its dominance over national economic growth for extended periods, then the risk of income polarization is very significant. To this must be added the reality of inherited wealth, which also grows faster than national output and wage income. The key implication is that, even if inequality in wage income were to be brought under control, overall inequality can continue to increase. So what kinds of solutions can be contemplated to tackle the imbalance in capital income and the policy treatment toward it?

Arguably the surest way to address some of these basic imbalances is through fiscal policy and particularly through more progressive taxation of capital gains and inherited wealth. While Piketty makes a case for a global tax on wealth, including inherited wealth, other economists call for capital income to be taxed at a higher rate than wage income. Of course, changes to fiscal policy for higher earners will run into vested interests and will require developing political consensus in the face of considerable entrenched power. A less contentious approach may involve helping to improve access to capital income for lower-income groups of workers above the wage incomes on which they are disproportionately reliant. Perhaps the most fundamental step would be to encourage savings to help accumulate wealth. Measures that can help here include improving financial inclusion by ensuring access to formal channels of finance, especially in countries with underdeveloped financial systems. Another is more widespread, or automatic, enrollment of workers in retirement plans with matching employer or government contributions to retirement savings accounts. Governments could also provide a guaranteed positive real rate of interest on the accumulated savings, as is done by Singapore's government-run Central Provident Fund. A more radical idea, which may help mitigate inheritance inequalities, is the introduction of a minimum inheritance for all, through, for example, child trust funds, with some contribution by government.[2]

Keeping with the idea of schemes organized through the workplace to support workers' gaining access to capital income, Robert Wade advanced the notion of companies forming trusts with the goal of paying dividends to the trust and in turn to the employee members of the trust. He suggested that companies could borrow on the capital markets and then engage in a form of internal lending to be paid to the employee members of the trust. Prudential measures, perhaps in the form of insurance, would need to be taken to ensure capital adequacy in order to repay the capital markets, but the balance of capital income generated could be paid out to the workers. How such a scheme may compare with other initiatives where companies aim to provide workers with a stake in the company's success in ways that go beyond wage income, such as profit sharing schemes for retirement or stock option plans, is certainly a broader debate worth having. On the surface, however, it would appear that an employer-directed and organized system may succeed in passing some small share of capital income on to the worker, but unless the source of the income becomes more diversified, it may run the risk of tying the worker further to the fate of the company. In the context of today's economy where most people entering the labor force are likely to have multiple careers and employers during their prime working years, the goal of increasing access for workers to capital income could run the risk of achieving minimal impact unless government does not involve itself in reconciling the many coordination problems and transactions costs that are likely to accompany such measures.

Policy and the role of government in an era of technology disruption

It has become commonplace to hear the attention given to the concept of "smart homes," "smart grids," "smart vehicles," "smart growth," "smart cities," and even "smart nations" these days. As the intersection between policy making, service delivery, and technology has been expanding significantly, new opportunities for the public sector are being created to also expand its capabilities, its reach, and its impact for the programs and services under its charge. At the same time, technological advance is very fast moving, often displacing existing practices and modes of producing and delivering services. This similarly presents challenges for governments to keep up with the pace of change in order to ensure adequate regulatory functions but also to act as an enabler for broader innovation and growth objectives. So, where can the role for government be appropriately situated amid such technological and digital transformation? As Ms. Jacqueline Poh, chief executive of the Government Technology Agency (GovTech) in Singapore, asked, whether the issue is making social services perform better for ordinary citizens or making business firms and industries achieve higher levels of productivity, the economic role of government can leverage its natural comparative advantage in three traditional areas but in new ways that could help governments better manage the many challenges and opportunities stemming from rapid change.

First, confronting the multifaceted infrastructure needs as it relates to broadband access, wireless mobility, and the Internet of things, is an important step. The convergence of these technologies is transforming what it means to have connectivity in advanced economies where the compression of time schedules for the delivery of high-value, nonroutine forms of work is a crucial risk factor (Smith, 1996; Fainstein, 2002; Sassen, 2012) in economic production, especially in global cities. As previously noted, even with regard to more conventional infrastructure such as bridges, roads, tunnels, and the like, investments made in many countries over the previous decades have been substantially lagging behind the demand and the needs for upgraded infrastructure systems. This is a problem that is most acute in the developing world, which is undergoing the most rapid population growth and urbanization. However, it is also a significant problem in advanced economies that struggle in managing the politics of public spending across fragmented political jurisdictions and multiple layers of government, as well as the problems of doing effective maintenance and rehabilitation of existing legacy systems. The World Economic Forum estimates global demand for infrastructure investment to be on the order of US\$3.7 trillion, while roughly US\$2.7 trillion is invested each year, leaving an annual deficit of US\$1 trillion, which corresponds to approximately 1.4% of global GDP (World Economic Forum, 2015). If these investment deficits persist or grow more significant, it is likely they will begin to erode future growth potential and productivity in a broad array of economic and social sectors.

Second is the issue of standards setting, which is an important part of enabling new technology-driven sectors to develop a fuller potential in the marketplace. Although the direction of technological advance in terms of market adoption is difficult to predict in this fast moving era of technological advance, the convergence of technology domains is increasing the need for standards that promote interoperability within and across technologies. Policy attention in this area is a crucial aspect of being able to scale up innovation that can unlock the productive potential of certain advances. Care must be taken, however, to ensure that standard setting is a substantially market driven and flexible process since the history of technological change contains numerous cases of inferior technologies gaining broad adoption and what economist W. Brian Arthur refers to as "lock-in" through what often amounts to accidents (Arthur, 1989; see also David, 1985, 1990). Government action as a standard setter or even as a strategic purchaser can significantly influence the direction of technology adoption and thus scalability, creating momentum to innovation in key areas but also retarding it in others.

Third, and related to the preceding area, is the notion of regulation, especially regulating for innovation and not against it. Standard setting must be accompanied by regulation, especially regulating for innovation, and not against it. Regulation plays a critical role in the adoption and spread of technologies. For example 3D printing would need approvals for materials that can be used in order to avoid toxicity and natural resource depletion. The regulation of utilities would help determine the impact of energy storage technologies. Changes in workplace regulations would be required to accommodate the growing ranks of gig workers – as discussed in Chapter 1. Regulations related to housing use would be needed to accommodate the demands of home owners and visitors who use home-sharing platforms like Airbnb and balance those demands against other social objectives.

When it comes to new growth industries characterized by an underlying science base that is rapidly evolving, collaborative processes are an important aspect of advancing technology development and commercialization outcomes. In such a context, it is important to consider the often interactive nature of innovative activity, predominately although not exclusively in R&D. An important facet of government regulation that affects this area is, of course, the intellectual property regime, especially through the patent system. Caught up in the policy discourse surrounding the role of government in creating an "attractive" business environment, particularly in the commercial and legal aspects, is the presumption that changes to the intellectual property regime should err on the side of stronger protection. Although from a purely rational standpoint this makes sense, what often gets downplayed is how it is fundamentally a system that bestows limited monopoly power on those innovators that finish first in sometimes costly patent races. At issue is how the current system in most advanced economies may not sufficiently recognize the extent to which innovation is the product of cumulative incremental contributions from multiple actors coming from many directions.[3] With all the efforts going into building smart cities and the platforms of technology that would necessarily accompany these types of programs, regulation in crucial areas of intellectual property protection must be seen as part of a broader objective of building a sustainable ecosystem of innovation that can support long-run economic growth.

Regulation and the push for competitive advantage

Continuing with the theme of regulation in the broader context of the role of government in the economy, how should one of government's traditional regulatory roles of making markets operate more efficiently be balanced with the pressures to help make economic sectors more competitive? In orthodox economic theory, market efficiency is synonymous with a zero or near zero profit condition yielding the textbook case of the perfectly competitive market. However, in the real world and its multiple factor and product markets, things seldom function in this manner. In fact, competitive advantage in certain industries is rather more associated with things that make markets operate less perfectly rather than more so. These include such well-known things as monopolization leading to predatory pricing, collusion among market actors that can produce price fixing or bid rigging, anticompetitive practices that create barriers to entry, dividing territories, bundling and tying of goods, lobbying for subsidies or tariff protection, among many others.

As much as these behaviors will remain a focus for government regulation of the economy, other factors influencing competitive advantage in today's growth industries tend strongly toward gaining an innovative edge. These are centered on securing access to specialized labor pools (including through immigration), gaining knowledge of industry road maps and the R&D direction of rivals, shortening R&D time horizons to finish first in patent races, and participating in networks of research and collaborative innovation that can lead to growth opportunities (Powell et al., 1996; von Hippel, 2002). Even as many are increasingly wondering whether America in particular may have a monopoly problem with many of its large technology firms, there is little doubt that entrenched market power has given companies like Amazon, Apple, Google, Microsoft, as well as others like AT&T, CISCO, and IBM before them (Bloomberg Business Week, 2017), distinct competitive advantages in shaping market structure and technological trajectories within economic sectors to their needs. Although a frequent refrain heard from these companies is that they are only one step away from having their entire business models and the underlying technology platform that runs them disrupted by the next great development, such competence-destroying innovation is hardly the norm in the broader history of technological advance (Rosenberg, 1976; Pavitt, 1984; Freeman, 1994; Cohen et al., 2000).

Nevertheless, the need for government to be able to preserve a level playing field for an innovation-driven economy crucially involves ensuring that Internet giants and other technology multinationals are not securing enduring advantages in the market through exploiting loopholes in order to circumvent unfavorable regulation (referred to as regulatory arbitrage). Another important aspect of supporting innovation as a driver of growth is helping to create a business environment, including the underlying cultural aspects of the economy and society, that supports risk capital and risk taking more broadly. What government regulation can do in this regard is the facilitation of access to capital, putting in place sound and streamlined business registration and bankruptcy laws, and the creation of an adequate supply of affordable space for innovation-led start-ups and small and medium-size enterprises (SMEs).

Dr. Beh Swan Gin, chair of Singapore's Economic Development Board (EDB), asserted how the dynamic growth in Asian markets is presenting new needs, many of which are not currently being met. Speaking about the large base of capabilities that the Singapore economy has built up, especially in the way its workforce is poised to take advantage of significant technological advances across the economy, the government remains focused on continuing to move Singapore beyond an investment-driven economy to one where the growth model is squarely centered on innovation. And echoing the comments made by Minister Ong at the outset, innovation means doing more with less (or at least doing more with the same) by originating new products and services that can address these unmet needs in the fast growing markets in Asia.

Today, given Singapore's openness, it is faced with the challenge of having to deal with antiglobalization forces as protectionist sentiments are on the rise in many OECD markets, and multinational companies are in turn rethinking how they operate according to Dr. Beh. Fortunately, Asian economies are growing fast, but Singapore needs to originate the new products and services to address the needs of Asian consumers, particularly the rising middle class, who are often different from those of consumers in the West. He further mentions how, if multinational companies or Singaporean companies are not developing the products and services to address that need, it is a near certainty that Indonesian companies will, Chinese companies will, or Indian companies will. So while there is opportunity, there is also a need for innovation to cater to new needs. That is why Singapore is moving away from an investment-driven economy to one that relies more on innovation. This requires continued outlays on R&D. It also requires attracting risk capital – not capital per se – but entrepreneurial skills, as well as design and creativity to foster innovation.

Cites, different levels of government, and the locus of innovation

If innovation is such a central part of development strategy for the future of the economy, it is important for policy to be attuned to some of its underlying characteristics such as where it tends to occur within national territories, and the social relations of production that propel it forward. Is innovation largely an urban-centered process? Certainly not exclusively, but there is ample evidence to suggest that most innovative activity is carried out not just in urban centers but within often very specific ones (Shearmur, 2012). Approximately one-half of the R&D being undertaken within OECD economies occurs in 10% of its regions (OECD, 2010), an illustration of its concentrated nature. Exhibiting strong local characteristics, it is important to recognize that innovation is an interactive, people-centered process that thrives in highly diverse and often collaborative environments, which is another reason that cities are uniquely well suited to be an important consideration for policy aimed at stimulating growth through innovation. This was a point of emphasis by Dr. John Powers, Research Fellow at the Lee Kuan Yew Centre for Innovative Cities at the Singapore University of Technology and Design. Citing how most cities and their local government leaders are generally understood to have limited power with regard to affecting the aggregate level of employment within their jurisdictions, since most employment is created at the level of the macroeconomy, cities thus focus on the work of attracting. Attracting capital investment, skilled labor, and any new functions that can lead to an expansion or diversification of the city's economic base. So, if innovation is widely perceived as a driver of long-run growth, what can cities do to positively influence innovation processes and innovation outcomes?

First is a recognition of the importance of education at all levels. Too often when discussing innovation, the focus as regards education is on the role of the research university and the applied sciences. There is little doubt this is a crucial aspect of promoting innovation in cities, as universities act as essential bridges to other innovation players. However, perhaps too little emphasis is placed on some of the foundational aspects of the education system within cities, particularly secondary schools where completion rates remain an important problem in many large cities in advanced economies. Second is the cultural aspect of innovation, especially entrepreneurship. Arguably cities' greatest asset is the diversity of people, occupations, skills, and modes of thinking that comprise them. Local government can play a crucial role in putting in place policies and programs that support trial and error, including the support of business failure and restarts. Another key area to expand the culture of innovation in cities is reducing barriers to improve the participation of women in the innovation economy. Third is a recognition of the importance of SMEs as an efficient employment generator and as a necessary tissue of economic activity that can help diversify the ecosystem of innovation and the economic base of cities over the long term. However, a key issue with the SME sector and its impact on innovation and economic development is the need for a critical mass of innovators in order to overcome the uncertainty and failure rates inherent in most forms of innovative activity and in making innovation a central organizing concept for urban economic development. Fourth is facilitating networks of collaboration pertinent to innovation. This can likely be done by drawing on regional assets in education, capital access, and customers but also through expanding ties between cities, which is where national and international research and contracting opportunities related to innovation are increasingly operating. Cities that are innovation leaders and those that hope to become more successful in promoting innovation must recognize that many of their firms are increasingly collaborating internationally and therefore should work to strengthen networks that are operative between cities. A focus on international student exchanges is a worthwhile place to start to build out such an initiative.

Notes

1 For a more complete discussion on how the rise in American income inequality has, at least over the last several decades, been substantially a product of policy rather than of pure market forces, see Stiglitz (2013).

2 Child trust funds were introduced in the UK in 2005, although they were discontinued in 2010. The idea was a long-term tax-free saving account to which parents could add a certain amount every year. The money would belong to the children, and they could take it out only when they reached 18 years of age.

3 The debate about the optimal strength of intellectual property protection regimes is one that is really quite tilted toward always stronger protection, even though evidence from multiple industries suggest that this in fact can prove stifling of innovative effort because of the winner-take-all aspects of most IP regimes. For useful insight into this debate, see Mazzoleni and Nelson (1998).

6 New challenges for the Asian developmental state

The thrust of this work and indeed the roundtable itself has clearly been directed at issues, problems, and opportunities facing advanced economies. Many, albeit not all, of the specific points raised here have been the product of research on emerging trends in large economies, with a particular emphasis on developments in places like the United States and Europe. In this concluding chapter, it is important to consider how some of these issues relate to the late industrializing economies of Asia, which, despite a slowdown, still remains among the most dynamic economic regions of the world.

The Asian region contains some of the world's most successful postwar cases of sustained economic development, including increases in living standards. Much of this growth and development has been substantially predicated on a catchup mode of economic development built around a unique form of state-mediated capitalism privileging relative openness, export orientation, and varying degrees of performance-driven industrial development and export targets in exchange for state subsidies and other protections (Johnson, 1982, 1995; Amsden, 1989, 2001; Haggard, 1990; Wade, 1990; Rodrik et al., 1995; Rodrik, 1997). Although the timing and specific contours of state–business relationships and the use of state power to propel industrial capability development has differed from country to country, these are some of the main lines of the Asian developmental state story, and they are rather well told. What is less understood, as it is an evolving process of transforming some of the economic institutions of some of the region's most successful economies, is how new economic policy making and governance can cope with the realities of needing to evolve growth through innovation and important aspects of economic and social disruption. Surely, this process has proceeded faster and further in some countries than in others with an overriding recognition that what has worked well in the recent past will not likely continue to work in the same way in the future.

The key question becomes how the developmental state organizes itself for a new set of economic and technological learning imperatives when by virtue of the nature of the uncertainties faced, government will need to be a more active alliance builder to a plurality of business firms and innovation actors than in preceding decades, when there was substantially more state-guided plan development around the main industrial trajectories for growth. In addition to the more heterogeneous and collaborative relationships inputting into the economic policy dialogue, the state will also have to contend with social cleavages that may be less acute than in many advanced Western economies but that are nevertheless a product of some of the same factors impacting these latter. These include globalization pressures linked to the rise of China; labor market and skills mismatches associated with sustained increases in tertiary education levels and a shifting industrial mix; socioeconomic disparities as a result of declining shares of national income going to the labor share as opposed to the owners of capital; and, perhaps most pertinent to several of the economies in the region as compared to the West, the multifaceted impacts of a rapidly aging society and workforce. Singapore faces variants of all these issues, as well as others that are unique to its open, foreign investment-driven, and land- and labor-constrained economy. As a city-state, the government wields far more power than most metropolitan regions around the world but also carries far more responsibility for its citizens and its workforce. Answers to these questions covering even some of Asia's most advanced economies would surely require considerably more in-depth analysis that is beyond the scope of this current project, but some treatment of the issues will concentrate on four main areas: restructuring of work and skill development; the pursuit of innovation as a pillar of economic growth; challenges to greater social inclusion; and new modes of governance thinking for economic development.

The changing nature of work

It seems nearly impossible these days to talk about changes in the labor force and the workplace more generally without hearing about all manner of disruption: How technology is automating jobs; how the share of national income going to labor has been on a perpetual decline in most economies; and how the expansion of nontraditional work arrangements through a proliferation of contracting and subcontracting, as well as the rise of gig workers for online platforms, has made the world of work a much more precarious situation for a great many. Even as demand for STEM-trained workers is high and only expected to increase, medium- and less-skilled workers face significant challenges in the years ahead. They risk either seeing their skills become outmoded by advances in technology or seeing their jobs undercut by more cost-effective temporary workers hired through third-party contractors. Significant concerns exist about the ability of advanced economies to create enough stable employment with adequate career ladders, even if there is widespread recognition that those entering the workforce today will need to prepare themselves for having multiple careers over the span of their working lives. In many Asian economies, such as Japan, Korea, and, perhaps to a lesser extent, Taiwan and Singapore, which have large corporate structures that have dominated significant segments of their economies, they have nonetheless privileged stable employment and continuous learning in the workplace (Best, 1990). How are some of these practices coming under pressure given the new realities discussed?

While virtually all of the advanced economies in Asia are highly educated, something that has long been thought to be not only a key source of competitive advantage but also a buffer against an economic downturn, restructuring in some key industries like electronics and advanced manufacturing in economies like Korea and Taiwan is beginning to show its longer-term effects of displacement. With cohort participation rates at over 40%, a level that Singapore is on track to reach by around 2020, these economies are currently having a more difficult time absorbing fresh graduates into the workforce with advanced degrees, either because the jobs being created are undershooting the skill level of new entrants to the labor force, the wages being paid are similarly inadequate for skilled workers, or both.[1] To some extent, these kinds of labor market mismatches and problems of the economy's absorptive capacity in a few key sectors, which had played such a prominent role in these economies' development, were perhaps inevitable to some degree.

In Singapore, where there have been sustained and significant labor shortages in the past and where persistent skills mismatches can present a serious problem for economic growth, the government is focused on trying to strike the right balance between increasing the supply of young graduates, particularly of STEM-trained graduates, and the need to think seriously about cultivating multiple paths to career success Government of Singapore, MTI, 2013b). Endowed with no natural resources of its own, the economy has operated ever since independence with the notion that its citizens are its greatest natural resource. A highly meritocratic structure has become a key feature of its education system and the civil service, but efforts are underway to broaden both degree and skill certification pathways so as to create a closer but multifaceted nexus between work and study. Singapore also uses a long-standing tripartite system of concertation between government, business, and the trade unions to address a range of economic matters, not the least of which is long-range planning for workforce skill development and employment facilitation. As it regards gig workers, the government is currently debating in Parliament the many different implications of this growing segment of the economy. In particular, what it means for the structure of benefits, particularly under Singapore's Central Provident Fund (its retirement/pension system), as well as how to provide health benefits for this class of freelance on-demand workers, which is something many other advanced economies have been quite slow to do.

Innovation-led growth

As economies all around the world, as well as many of the cities within their national territories, are scrambling to stake their claim on the global innovation landscape, great competition and also great cooperation are occurring simultaneously. Cities compete to attract talent perhaps more than ever before (Florida, 2007), but R&D work is also increasingly internationalizing (von Zedtwitz and Gassmann, 2002), including the manner in which firms structure cross-border collaboration pertaining to R&D (OECD, 2010). Given the many contingent place-bound characteristics that make certain places hotbeds for innovation, the emphasis on cities as a locus of innovative effort is not misguided, even though it remains an unanswered question as to the extent to which, and in what ways exactly, innovation may be a distinctively urban phenomenon (Shearmur, 2012). Many of the Asian economies are certainly not newcomers to investing in R&D, with gross expenditure on R&D (GERD) in the upper range of national performers when compared to all OECD nations. From Japan and Korea, to Taiwan and Singapore, as well as China, many Asian economies have all been significantly upgrading or at least maintaining their already significant commitment to R&D (Government of Singapore, A*STAR, 2013a). However, R&D spend only tells part of the story with regard to innovation and long-run economic growth.

A key part of the innovation story is what drives an innovative culture, as alluded to in the previous chapter, which in turn produces critical mass on both the input side (R&D) and on the output side. The latter can range from scientific papers and patents to firm formation and commercializable technologies and their broader adoption in the market. Singapore is an interesting case in that close to 30 years since its major push into R&D began, the government continues to sustain a major commitment to innovative effort, recently announcing a new S$19 billion funding effort for R&D over the next five years. However, in many ways the payoffs on the output side have lagged behind the investments and policy measures made on the input side (Thampuran and Kong, 2016). It is not easy to pinpoint the reasons for this, but they range from the manner in which career aspirations are being formed in an economy where the cohort participation rate has climbed to 32% and is on track to reach 40% in the next few years[2] to whether a surplus of potential public incentive and subsidy schemes may be distorting innovative outcomes (*Financial Times*,

8 May 2017). On this latter, one of the key differentiators for the success of the developmental state in Asia, as opposed to many other late industrializing countries, has been the way government and business have operated within what Amsden (2001) has called a "reciprocal control mechanism," broadly pertaining to the (performance-based) principles that govern subsidy allocation or access to other selective government incentives. How elements of such a mechanism can be adapted to the context of innovative entrepreneurship of a more frontier variety in the future has great bearing on innovation outcomes, including scale effects.

The case of Israel and Taiwan are of importance here in the way that more exacting standards have been implemented with how firms are pushed to develop and adopt more advanced technology in exchange for access to government funding schemes or being allowed to operate within government-administered science parks (Mathews, 2002; Amsden and Chu, 2003; Breznitz, 2007). More stringent standards, however, are likely to succeed only if there is a stronger uptake of innovation and entrepreneurship as a career path in a place like Singapore. This is something Minister Ong Ye Kung pointed out at the beginning of the roundtable, in that developing a viable culture of innovation must embrace trial and error and all it implies in terms of business success and business failure.

Issues with social inclusion

Third, it is partly a by-product of the relatively more recent industrialization and economic modernization drives in several late industrializing Asian economies that socioeconomic and income polarization has not reached the high levels observed in a growing number of major Western economies. There is also little doubt that virtually none of Asia's most advanced economies have ever adopted many of the defining features of an Anglo-American style of market organization that is characterized by a more neo-liberal orientation in the way that private market incentives are infused into fiscal policy, capital–labor relationships, corporate governance, decentralized decision making, and significant political pressure to increased public spending on programs of social uplift. Certainly more restrained social conventions around corporate governance have moderated wealth accumulation at the upper tiers of the income distribution in many of the advanced Asian economies such as Japan, Korea, Taiwan, and elsewhere, compared to the rest of the OECD, such that income inequality may not be the most pertinent area in which to address some of the more pressing issues regarding social inclusion.

One of the key issues regarding economic and social development and the reciprocal tensions that may exist between them is urbanization and the patterns of urban development from large cities to mega cities. Of the top 20 mega cities in the world today, typically defined as having a metropolitan regional population of over 10 million people, 14 of them are in Asia. Of these, eight can be considered to be within some of Asia's most advanced economies, including rapidly rising China. Much of this is the result of internal migration from rural areas to already large cities or from smaller urban areas to the country's largest cities, compared to higher levels of immigration that are driving much urban population expansion in Western economies, albeit at rates that are slowing (United Nations, 2017b). This is placing considerable pressure on the physical fabric of cities in terms of transportation, housing, sanitation, and other critical systems, as well as the social infrastructure pertaining to education, health care, and labor markets. Even as citizens of the country in which they are migrating toward the large urban centers, it is common that they do not always have the same rights to the city in terms of accessing some of this physical and social infrastructure. The case of China's "hukou" (household registration) system, which regulates important access rights to housing and other key social services in Chinese cities, is rather well documented (Yusuf and Wu, 1997; Wu et al., 2007), but similar restrictions also exist in Indonesia. The need to devise new partnerships to support the integration of migrants in large Asian cities will be a crucial step in stimulating economic growth in overburdened large cities, as well as reducing poverty on an urban and national scale (Deshingkar, 2006).

Another challenge to social inclusion in some of Asia's more advanced economies has to do with the multifaceted issue of aging and what this means for the workforce and for society in an era of rapid and accelerating technological change. Advanced economies like Japan, Korea, and Singapore, among several others, will be facing significant issues in the years ahead as the proportion of the population aged 60 years and older will be growing at exceedingly high rates. For instance, according to a report by the United Nations (2015), Korea is projected to have a 77% increase in its population aged 60 and above over the period 2015–2030. In the case of Singapore, this figure rises to an extraordinary 97% over the same period. For a country that is already significantly labor constrained, this invites serious questions as to the ability to grow the labor force, its impact on the pace of job creation, and the adequacy of the skills base given the twin realities of rapid technical advance and a likely increasing reliance on older workers. In the government's own Population White Paper (Government of Singapore, NPTD, 2013c), the demographic projections point to more labor force exits than entrants by 2030 implying significant difficulties in the years ahead in terms of sustaining a vibrant economy on the basis of the resident population. Already having some of the highest labor force participation rates in the world,[3] Singapore will have to confront a difficult reality in addressing the practical limitations to pushing these rates higher still in the interest of maintaining an active labor force. With the retirement age recently nudged upward to 67 (referred to as the re-employment age) and with talk of edging higher still in the years ahead and many working well beyond retirement age, it is reasonable to ask what it means to retire in Singapore, and, conversely, what it means to be a part of the older workforce in an economy that will likely be more dependent on them. Singapore and other advanced economies such as Japan and, to a lesser extent, Korea have shown either increasing (Singapore) or long-standing (Japan) domestic political resistance to growing the proportion of foreign workers in the economy or toward higher levels of outright immigration. Therefore, if growth must derive, at least in substantial measure, from an aging workforce, the key question then becomes what social policies promote continuous learning and skill upgrading, as well as developing meaningful workplace practices that integrate and value older workers and their experience and that facilitate knowledge exchange in multiple directions.

Governance and the economic institutions of the developmental state

Has the basic economic problem, as posed by Amsden 1989, (2001) pertaining to the nature of late industrialization and what she refers to as the developmental imperative of building "knowledge-based assets" through reciprocal control in state–business relationships, been resolved? Much of this involves being able to develop and grow economically in a unique historical context of overcoming the need to industrialize in an era in which most industrial technology has already been commercialized by large firms in advanced regions, thus creating a further need to be able to industrialize without proprietary innovations. As regards the modes of governance, specifically the economic role of government for long-term economic development, even though it is difficult to generalize across even the most successful late industrializing economies of Asia, it is possible to say that they have perhaps never adopted the kind of free market approaches that exist in Anglo-American–style economies in the West. Differing degrees of state-mediated capitalism have existed alongside a probusiness and export-oriented system. Industrialization drives throughout successive periods extending back to the 1960s and 1970s in Korea, Taiwan, and Singapore have all been characterized by high levels of long-range economic planning, industrial targeting, and state–business relationships that have reflected some degree of what Krugman (1986, 1990) has called "strategic trade." These characteristics have many subtleties to them and have certainly not remained constant in either their nature or the extent of state involvement over the intervening years. Nevertheless, it is difficult to ignore many of the basic contours of a top-down system of economic policy making that has prioritized industrial upgrading centered heavily on mastery of new industrial technologies and proprietary innovation (Kim and Nelson, 2000; Amsden, 2001).

Irrespective of the hybrid forms government and private sector involvement in some of the now developed economies of Asia, a critical challenge going forward will be how governments are less likely to be the effective resource allocators and the definers of industrial trajectories in the ways that have worked so well in the past. It further means that many of the selective interventions used to propel firms down technological learning curves in earlier decades of catchup industrialization, as has been done with sometimes great effect in Taiwan and Korea in particular,[4] are not likely to be as productive in the context of having to innovate at or near the world technological frontier. Surely, this is well understood among the successful economies of Asia, including China, which have all been engaged in shifting away from some of these trademark forms of selective intervention and technological guidance – some of which have penetrated into the managerial decisions of firms – that were instrumental to economic development, and instead are embracing new modes of governance for economic development. This point was made by Mr. Peter Ho, the former head of the civil service in Singapore and current chair of the Urban Redevelopment Authority, during a series of lectures given at the Institute of Policy Studies of the National University of Singapore on the occasion of being named this year's S.R. Nathan Fellow.[5] He squarely put the focus on government's need to be adaptable to ensure that economies and the specific centers of innovation within them develop or retain a place of centrality within increasingly global networks of innovation and production. Basically, complexity and the democratization of much industrial knowledge have converged to create a situation where government planners are increasingly unable to monopolize the kind of information they used in the context of the developmental state. This in turn requires a much more significant orientation toward active engagement with business, innovators, communities, educators, and students, and with civil society more broadly, in ways that have not traditionally been a hallmark of the institutional arrangements for economic development in many Asian economies. What this might mean for the top-down style of economic planning that has been a hallmark of the Asian developmental state and that persists in very important ways especially in Singapore today is one of the main governance challenges in the years ahead. Although tripartite structures among government, employers, and the trade unions are a big part of the long-range planning process in a number of key areas such as strategic manpower planning, skills and education, and even wage consultations, it is likely that new forms of citizen and private sector engagement will need to be a bigger part of the economic role of government and economic planning going forward. The high degree of trust that many of these Asian developmental states have garnered over the years, particularly here in Singapore, in being effective stewards of the economic development process will likely need to begin to flow outward from government to new segments of the economy and society, particularly to a new and more diverse set of innovation actors to be able to chart new directions and deliver growth performance.

Notes

1 This information was provided in a personal interview with a senior official for Singapore's Ministry of Education in February 2016 and is consistent with recent researched by the World Bank; see Almeida et al. (2012).
2 A nontrivial factor in this regard is Singapore's dominant financial services and advanced producer services industry, which is a great attractor of young Singaporean graduates, many of them trained in STEM fields. "The Future of the Economy" study, mentioned in the introduction, made an effort to study the connection between degree type and occupational choice for recent university graduates in Singapore in an effort to better understand how the weighty financial services industry may be impacting career choice. The data was difficult to come by as it required the various public universities to share data on their graduates, but the investigations, however tentative, were consistent with considerable anecdotal evidence that the higher salaries and prestige effects associated with jobs in the financial services industry are an important variable in the way young skilled Singaporeans are forming their career aspirations. The extent to which this has the potential to have a dampening effect on Singapore's entrepreneurial innovation economy is an important question that requires additional study. For further discussion of this and related issues, see Powers (with Jayasakera and Hong), forthcoming.
3 The data from the Ministry of Manpower for 2013 shows that for males 60–64, the labor force participation rate is 75%, for males 65–69, it is 53%, and for those 70–74, it is 36%, and, finally, for those 75 and above, it is 13%. For women, these rates are lower but still quite high by international standards.
4 In the case of Taiwan, see Mathews (2002) and Amsden and Chu (2003). For Korea, see Amsden (1989, 2001) and Rodrik et al. (1995).
5 The point raised here comes from his fourth lecture entitled "The Future Governance: Unintended Consequences and the Redemption of Hope," delivered in May 2017.

References

Acemoglu, Daron; Autor, David; Dorn, David; Hanson, Gordon H.; and Price, Brendan, 2014, "Return of the Solow Paradox? IT, Productivity, and Employment in US Manufacturing," *American Economic Review: Papers and Proceedings*, Vol. 104, No. 5, pgs. 394–9.

Almeida, Rita; Behrman, Jere; and Cobalino, David (eds.), 2012, *The Right Skills for the Job? Re-thinking Training Policies for Workers*, World Bank, Washington, DC.

Amsden, Alice H., 1989, *Asia's Next Giant: South Korea and Late Industrialization*, Oxford University Press, New York.

———, 1994, *The Market Meets Its Match: Restructuring the Economies of Eastern Europe*, Harvard University Press, Cambridge, MA.

———, 2001, *The Rise of the Rest: Challenges to the West From Late Industrializing Economies*, Oxford University Press, New York.

Amsden, Alice H.; and Chu, Wan-wen, 2003, *Beyond Late Development: Taiwan's Upgrading Policies*, MIT Press, Cambridge, MA.

Arthur, W. Brian, 1989, "Competing Technologies, Increasing Returns, and Lock-in by Historical Events," *Economic Journal*, Vol. 99 (March), pgs. 116–31.

ASCE (American Society of Civil Engineers), 2016, "Failure to Act: Closing the Infrastructure Investment Gap for America's Economic Future," ASCE, Reston, VA.

Autor, David H.; Levy, Frank; and Murnane, Richard J., 2003, "The Skill Content of Recent Technological Change," *Quarterly Journal of Economics*, Vol. 118, No. 4, pgs. 1279–333.

Bebchuck, Lucian; and Fried, Jesse, 2004, *Pay Without Performance: The Unfulfilled Promise of Executive Compensation*, Harvard University Press, Cambridge, MA.

Best, Michael, 1990, *The New Competition: Institutions of Industrial Restructuring*, Harvard University Press, Cambridge, MA.

Bloomberg Business Week, 2017, "Should America's Tech Giants Be Broken Up?" by Paula Dwyer (20 July).

Breznitz, Dan, 2007, *Innovation and the State: Political Choice and Strategies for Growth in Israel, Taiwan, and Ireland*, Yale University Press, New Haven, CT.

Brynjolfsson, Erik; and McAfee, Andrew, 2011, *Race Against the Machine: How the Digital Revolution Is Accelerating Innovation, Driving Productivity, and Irreversibly Transforming Employment and the Economy*, Digital Frontier Press, Lexington, MA.

Case, Anne; and Deaton, Angus, March 2017, "Mortality and Morbidity in the 21st Century," Brookings Papers on Economic Activity, Washington, DC.

Castells, Manuel, 1989, *The Informational City: Information Technology, Economic Restructuring, and the Urban-regional Process*, Basil Blackwell, Oxford.

Cohen, Wesley M.; Nelson, Richard R.; and Walsh, John P., 2000, "Protecting Their Intellectual Assets: Appropriability Conditions and Why US Manufacturing Firms Patent (or Not)," NBER Working Paper No. 7552, National Bureau of Economic Research, Cambridge, MA.

David, Paul A., 1985, "Clio and the Economics of QWERTY," *American Economic Review*, Vol. 75, No. 2 (May), pgs. 332–7.

———, 1990, "The Dynamo and the Computer: An Historical Perspective on the Modern Productivity Paradox," *American Economic Review*, Vol. 80, No. 2 (May), pgs. 355–61.

DePillis, Lydia, 2016, "Department of Labor Sends Warning Shot to Clients of Temp Staffing Agencies," *Washington Post Wonkblog*, January 20.

Deshingkar, Priya, 2006, "Internal Migration, Poverty, and Development in Asia," Paper presented for the Asia 2015 Conference Hosted by the Institute of Development Studies and the Overseas Development Institute, UK.

Dewar, Margaret; and Manning Thomas (eds.), June 2012, *The City After Abandonment*, University of Pennsylvania Press, Philadelphia.

Donovan, Sarah A.; Labonte, Marc; and Dalaker, Joseph, 2016, "The US Income Distribution: Trends and Issues," Congressional Research Service, United States Congress, Washington, DC.

Economist, 2015, "Why American Wage Growth Is So Lousy?" (14 April).

Economist, 2016, "Automation and Anxiety" (25 June).

Fainstein, Susan S., 2002, "The Changing World Economy and Urban Restructuring," in Campbell, Scott, and Fainstein, Susan S. (eds.), *Readings in Urban Theory*, Blackwell Publishers, London.

———, 2010, *The Just City*, Cornell University Press, Ithaca, NY.

Financial Times, 2017, "Singapore Start-ups Spark Query Over Quality," by Jeevan Vasagar (8 May).

Fishman, Robert, 1987, *Bourgeois Utopias: The Rise and Fall of Suburbia*, Basic Books, New York.

Florida, Richard, 2007, *The Flight of the Creative Class: The New Global Competition for Talent*, Harper Collins, New York.

Frank, Malcom; Roehrig, Paul; and Pring, Ben, 2017, *What to Do When Machines Do Everything? How to Get Ahead in a World of AI, Algorithms, Bots, and Big Data*, Wiley & Sons, Hoboken, NJ.

Freeman, Chris, 1994, "The Economics of Technical Change," *Cambridge Journal of Economics*, Vol. 18 (October), pgs. 463–514.

Gardner, Sarah, 2016, "Why Careers Are Gone, and Jobs Are Going Next," *Marketplace – Business Insider*, June 17.

Glaeser, Edward, 2011, *The Triumph of the City: How Our Greatest Invention Makes Us Richer, Smarter, Greener, Healthier, and Happier*, Macmillan, Oxford.

Government of New York City, n.d., "Sandy and Its Impacts," www.nyc.gov/html/sirr/downloads/pdf/final_report/Ch_1_SandyImpacts_FINAL_singles.pdf

Government of Singapore, 2013a, "National Survey of R&D in Singapore," Agency for Science, Technology and Research, A*STAR, Singapore.

————, 2013b, "Population and Economy," Ministry of Trade and Industry, Occasional Paper, Singapore.

————, 2013c, "A Sustainable Population for a Dynamic Singapore (Population White Paper)," National Population and Talent Division, Singapore.

Haggard, Stephan, 1990, *Pathways From the Periphery: The Politics of Growth in the Newly Industrializing Countries*, Cornell University Press, Ithaca, NY.

Halonen-Akatwijuka, Maija; and Oliver Hart, 2016, "Continuing Contracts," August, https://scholar.harvard.edu/files/hart/files/continuing_contracts_august25_2016-1.pdf

Healey, Patsy, 1992, "Planning Through Debate: The Communicative Turn in Planning Theory," *The Town Planning Review*, Vol. 63, No. 2 (April), pgs. 143–62.

————, 1997, *Collaborative Planning*, Macmillan, Houndmills, Basingstoke, Hampshire.

Ho, Peter, 2017, "The Challenges of Governance in a Complex World, Lecture IV – The Future: Governance, Unintended Consequences and the Redemption of Hope," Lecture given as the 2016–17 S.R. Nathan Fellow for the Study of Singapore, Institute of Policy Studies-Nathan Lectures, National University of Singapore (NUS), Singapore (17 May).

IDB, 2014, "Medellin: A City Transformed," Inter-American Development Bank, Washington, DC, www.iadb.org/en/topics/citizen-security/impact-medellin,5687.html

ILO, 2016, "Global Wage Report 2016/17: Wage Inequality in the Workplace," International Labour Organization, Geneva, Switzerland.

IMF, 2016, "Article IV Consultation – The Peoples' Republic of China – IMF Country Report," International Monetary Fund, Washington, DC.

Information Technology and the US Workforce: Where Are We and Where Do We Go From Here? April 2017. National Academies Press, Washington, DC.

Infrastructure for the 21st Century: Framework for a Research Agenda. 1987. National Academy of Sciences, Washington, DC.

Johnson, Chalmers, 1982, *MITI and the Japanese Miracle: The Growth of Industrial Policy*, 1925–1975, Stanford University Press, Palo Alto, CA.

Johnson, Chalmers, 1995, *Japan: Who Governs? The Rise of the Developmental State*, W.W. Norton and Co., New York, NY.

Katz, Lawrence F.; and Krueger, Alan B., 2016, "The Rise and Nature of Alternative Work Arrangements in the United States, 195–2015," NBER Working Paper 22667, National Bureau of Economic Research, Cambridge, MA.

Kim, Linsu; and Nelson, Richard R. (eds.), 2000, *Technology, Learning, and Innovation: Experiences of Newly Industrializing Countries*, Cambridge University Press, Cambridge.

Kravis, Irving B., 1970, "Trade as a Handmaiden of Growth: Similarities between the Nineteenth and Twentieth Centuries," *Economic Journal*, Vol. 80, No. 320 (December), pgs. 850–72.

Krugman, Paul (ed.), 1986, *Strategic Trade Policy and the New International Economics*, MIT Press, Cambridge, MA.

————, 1990, *Rethinking International Trade*, MIT Press, Cambridge, MA.

Mathews, John A., 2002, "The Origins and Dynamics of Taiwan's R&D Consortia," *Research Policy*, Vol. 31, pgs. 633–51.

Mazzoleni, Roberto; and Nelson, Richard R., 1998, "The Benefits and Costs of Strong Patent Protection: A Contribution to the Current Debate," *Research Policy*, Vol. 27, No. 3, pgs. 273–84.

McKinsey Global Institute, 2016a, "Bridging Global Infrastructure Gaps" (June).

McKinsey Global Institute, 2017, "Jobs Lost, Jobs Gained: workforce transitions in a time of automation," (December).

———, 2016b, "Poorer Than Their Parents? Flat or Falling Incomes in Advanced Economies" (July).

Nelson, Richard R. and Winter, Sidney G., 1982, *An Evolutionary Theory of Economic Change*, The Belknap Press of Harvard University, Cambridge, MA.

OECD, 2010, "Innovation to Strengthen Growth and Address Global and Social Challenges: Key Findings," Ministerial Report on the OECD Innovation Strategy, OECD, Paris, France.

Pavitt, Keith, 1984, "Sectoral Patterns of Technical Change: Towards a Taxonomy and a Theory," *Research Policy*, Vol. 13, pgs. 343–73.

Piketty, Thomas, 2013, *Capital in the Twenty First Century*, Belknap Press of Harvard University Press, Cambridge, MA.

Powell, Walter; Koput, Kenneth; and Smith-Doerr, Laurel, 1996, "Interorganizational Collaboration and the Locus of Innovation: Networks of Learning in Biotechnology," *Administrative Science Quarterly*, Vol. 41, pgs. 116–45.

Powers, John C., 2013, "'Un-traded Interdependencies' as a Useful Theory of Regional Economic Development: A Comparative Study of Innovation in Dublin and Beijing," Unpublished PhD dissertation, Graduate School of Arts and Sciences, Columbia University, New York, NY.

Rabianski, Joseph S.; and Clements, J. Sherwood, 2007, "Mixed-use Development: A Review of Professional Literature," Prepared for the National Association of Industrial and Office Properties Research Foundation, Herndon, VA.

Rinaldi, Steven; Peerenboom, James; and Kelly, Terrence, 2001, "Identifying, Understanding, and Analyzing Critical Infrastructure Interdependencies," *The Institute of Electrical and Electronics Engineers, IEEE Control Systems Magazine*, Vol. 21, pgs. 11–25.

Rodrik, Dani, 1997, "Trade Strategy, Investment and Exports: Another Look at East Asia," *Pacific Economic Review*, Vol. 2, No. 1, pgs. 1–24.

Rodrik, Dani; Grossman, Gene; and Norman, Victor, 1995, "Getting Interventions Right: How South Korea and Taiwan Grew Rich," *Economic Policy*, Vol. 20 (April), pgs. 53–107.

Rosenberg, Nathan, 1976, "The Direction of Technological Change: Inducement Mechanisms and Focusing Devices," in Rosenberg, Nathan (ed.), *Perspectives on Technology*, Cambridge University Press, Cambridge.

———, 1996, "Uncertainty and Technological Change," in Landau, R. et al. (eds.), *The Mosaic of Economic Growth*, Stanford University Press, Palo Alto, CA.

Sassen, Saskia, 2012, *Cities in a World Economy* (4th edition), Sage Publications, Thousand Oaks, CA.

Shearmur, Richard, 2012, "Are Cities the Font of Innovation? A Critical Review of the Literature on Cities and Innovation," *Cities*, Vol. 29, pgs. S9–S18.

Smith, Neil, 1996, *The New Urban Frontier: Gentrification and the Revanchist City*, Routledge, New York.

Stiglitz, Joseph E., 2002, *Globalization and Its Discontents*, W.W. Norton & Company, New York.

———, 2003, "Globalization and the Economic Role of the State in the New Millennium," *Industrial and Corporate Change*, Vol. 12, No. 1, pgs. 3–26.

———, 2013, *The Price of Inequality: How Today's Divided Society Endangers Our Future*, W.W. Norton & Company, New York.

Straits Times, 2016, "Globalisation and Its New Discontents," Opinion piece by Joseph E. Stiglitz (8 August).

"Technology, Jobs and the Future of Work," 2017, Briefing note prepared for the Fortune Vatican Forum [updated February].

Thampuran, Raj; and Kong, Hwai Loong, 2016, "The Biomedical Sciences: Research for Better Health," in Hang, Chang Chieh; Low, Teck Seng; and Thampuran, Raj (eds.), *The Singapore Research Story*, World Scientific, Singapore.

United Nations, 2017a, *World Population Ageing – 2015*, Department of Economic and Social Affairs, New York.

———, June 2017b, *World Population Prospects: The 2017 Revision*, Department of Economic and Social Affairs, New York.

U.S. Bureau of the Census, 2015, *American Community Survey*, Bureau of the Census, Suitland, MD.

von Hippel, Eric, 2002, "Horizontal Innovation Networks – By and for Users," MIT Sloan School of Management Working Paper, No. 4366-02, Cambridge, MA.

von Zedtwitz, Maximilian and Gassmann, Oliver, 2002, "Market Versus Technology Drive in R&D Internationalization: Four Different Patterns of Managing Research and Development," *Research Policy*, Vol. 31, pgs. 569–88.

Wade, Robert, 1990, *Governing the Market: Economic Theory and the Role of Government in East Asian Industrialization*, Princeton University Press, Princeton, NJ.

Wall Street Journal, 2015, "Wage-Law Enforcer Favours Proactive Approach," by Lauren Weber (21 March).

Wardner, Pamela, 2014, "Explaining Mixed-Use Developments: A Critical Realist's Perspective," Paper presented at the 20th Annual Pacific-Rim Real Estate Society Conference, 19–22 January, Christchurch, New Zealand.

Weil, David, 2014, *The Fissured Workplace: Why Work Has Become So Bad for So Many and What Can Be Done to Improve It*, Harvard University Press, Cambridge, MA.

Wilkinson, Richard; and Pickett, Kate, 2009, *The Spirit Level: Why More Equal Societies Almost Always Do Better*, Allen Lane, London.

World Economic Forum, 2015, "The Global Competitiveness Report," Klaus Scwab (ed.), World Economic Forum, Geneva, Switzerland.

World Bank, 2016, "Global Infrastructure Facility," www.worldbank.org/en/programs/global-Infrastructure-facility

Wright, Frank Lloyd, 1932, *The Disappearing City*, W.F. Payson, New York.

Wu, Fulong; Xu, Jiang; and Yeh, Anthony, 2007, *Urban Development in Post-Reform China: State, Market, and Space*, Routledge, Abingdon.

Yusuf, Shahid; and Wu, Weiping, 1997, *The Dynamics of Urban Growth in Three Chinese Cities*, The World Bank, Oxford University Press, New York.

Index